"Teresa DeCicco articulates cle
exploration of transformation,
insider's perspective: as a woman who's experienced the richness
of life beyond the five senses."
—Lisa Wimberger, author of *New Beliefs, New Brain*

"Spiritual insight at its best. Teresa DeCicco does a masterful job
of reminding us that we are not alone in our profound journey of
personal spiritual transformation."
—Cynthia Banks, documentary filmmaker, Banks Productions
Limited

"Just as a caterpillar goes through intense physiological changes
in its journey toward becoming a butterfly, so do our senses
undergo refinement, during our own spiritual and biological
transformation. *Living Beyond the Five Senses* is a beautiful and
practical roadmap for the emerging human butterfly."
—Kiara Windrider, author of *Year Zero: Time of the Great Shift*,
and *Ilahinoor: Awakening the Divine Human*

"In *Living Beyond the Five Senses*, Teresa has created a practical
spirituality that is useful as well as inspiring for everyday life."
—Melinda Hynes ICADC, EFT practitioner

"This book will guide readers to find a way to heal emotionally
and to experience peace and joy, regardless of the issue that they
have to work on. By setting a conscious commitment to live life
mindfully, by using our dreams, body information, thoughts, and
emotions, we will find that life is really amazing."
—Maria N. Gallo, MA, RMFT, psychotherapist at Family Service
Thames Valley, London, Ontario

"The book speaks about all the self-care behaviors I am practicing and encouraging my clients to practice as well, and how I can improve my practices. We are in need of doing the "work" from the inside out, whatever that "work" is for us as individuals. Welcome, *Homo nuovo!* I plan on making this book a regular tune-up for my spiritual well-being."
—**Heather Amisson ICADC, family counselor**

"What a great read! People often ask me how they can learn to tune in or connect with the spirit world . . . and this book is a fantastic resource to do just that!"
—**Linda Ouellet, psychic medium, author:** *A Soul Comes Home* and *Mind of a Medium*

"I have been a student of two books since I sobered up eight years ago: *The Big Book of Alcoholics Anonymous* and *The Spirituality of Imperfection*. This book, *Living Beyond the Five Senses*, has been life-changing and will be forever added to my spiritual walk forward."
—**Kevin Amisson ICADC, CTRTC Manager, Renascent Paul J. Sullivan Centre**

ACKNOWLEDGMENTS

This book has come to life because many people believed that I could be the purveyor of this news. People invested their time and skills, asked for nothing in return, and for this I am deeply grateful. A few who have gone above and beyond what was needed of them are mentioned here.

Words cannot express the gratitude I have for Heather Higgins who helped with the editing and shaping of this book. We have lived parallel lives and for this reason, she understood what I wanted to say and encouraged me to say it.

Nicolle Miller, who excitedly embraced the topic, even though it was foreign ground to her; I am so appreciative of her enthusiasm and openness to read the first draft and provide valuable feedback. It was through her youthful and inquisitive eyes that I was able to approach the book in a new way.

My sons, Matthew and Anthony, whom I thank beyond measure, for they have been the greatest teachers of love. Thank you to Walt Gibson, for without him this book would not exist; he provides the perfect mirror for my own reflection, which then begs me to make the journey inward.

To Michael Wiese and all those at Divine Arts who put their immense talent, time, and effort into this book. Since I have no skill in the art of bookmaking I put this entirely in their hands and they created something that is greater than any one of us could have done alone; thank you for sharing this adventure with me.

TABLE OF CONTENTS

PART I

The Spiritual Transformation of Humans

PROLOGUE

A SIXTEEN-YEAR-OLD BOY finds himself in excruciating abdominal pain accompanied by nausea, fatigue, and internal bleeding. Over the course of several weeks his condition progressively worsens to the point where he can no longer eat or even speak. The boy is hospitalized with a team of doctors overlooking his dire condition while attempting to solve his failing health problems.

One day, the boy asks to be taken to the atrium of the hospital, which is streaming with bright, warm sunlight. As he sits in his wheelchair in a feeble state, with his face absorbing the light, he begins to transcend everything around him and he suddenly sees and feels a world that cannot be seen with the eyes alone. This is the world within the world. As he is swept away by the experience, he suddenly understands the great mystery of life and why he is on the planet. Shortly thereafter, he finds himself possessing extremely creative talents, clairvoyant abilities, and, during sleep, he is guided by dreams that foretell his future.

In time, the medical team is able to stabilize his physical condition and he is released from the hospital to return home to resume his life. His life, however, is no longer the one he knew prior to entering the hospital. Though one young man entered the hospital, a completely transformed one was released; only in physical appearance were they similar. This young man is one of millions of people from all walks of life, from all ages and cultures, and in a multitude of ways, undergoing the transformation to Spiritual Beings. *Living Beyond the Five Senses* is both a description and an invitation to this life-changing process for anyone wishing to embark on the grand adventure.

CHAPTER 1

WHAT IS *HOMO NUOVO*?

———

This chapter is dedicated to all the children who
have touched my life and have shown me true joy;
they are the next generation of *Homo nuovo*.

A SUBTLE CURRENT has been flowing through the human race since the beginning of time and though the change has been very gradual, it has been constant and unrelenting. This change has been occurring in the human population like a drop of water dripping on a massive rock cliff. The drip works gently but eventually the rock cracks open and the inside is revealed. This parallels the change in humans who gradually, over time, have been transformed by a constant force of pressure. A Spiritual Being, one that has conscious awareness beyond the self and beyond the five senses, has now emerged in the human race in vast numbers. This human, or *Homo nuovo* as it has been coined, is the result of spiritual teachings and shifts that have been occurring for millennia. This human is a natural extension of the long line of early humans such as *Homo erectus*, to those who then became the current humans, *Homo sapiens,* to the new race discussed herein as *Homo nuovo*.

Though it has been said for many years that the time has come, or a new age is upon us, proof that the time is now, is evident. The proof is in the vast number of humans who are now consciously aware of a life beyond the self, one that is intricately connected to all things in the universe. These humans are also aware that they are in fact participating in reality with thoughts, feelings, and behaviors. The subtle momentum has done its work to the point where spiritual transformation over time has resulted in the emergence of Spiritual Beings.

Each of the religious prophets, meditation and yoga movements proliferating around the world, information about spirituality being shared around the globe so quickly and easily, popular culture seeding spiritual messages in music, film, and art, are all credited for contributing to this profound change in humans. These were the drops of water that fell quietly and forcefully upon consciousness, which then shaped and changed it until a Spiritual Being emerged.

Before delving deeply into the process and outcomes of this Spiritual Being three terms need to be defined as they are used in the context of this book; these terms are *transformation, spirituality*, and *religion*. When the term transformation is used this refers to a *process of change* that can occur slowly or very rapidly, depending on each person and the circumstances that occur. This transformation or growth process occurs for each person at the physical, emotional, mental, and spiritual levels. This process may not actually be occurring at random but the foundations for these changes will not be the focus of this book. The theories as to why this process occurs are highly varied, and are in themselves a separate matter for discussion. The focus of this book is the process itself and how it unfolds. The premise of this book recognizes that spiritual transformation is occurring in humans and either consciously or unconsciously, the changes are ensuing.

In terms of these changes, the distinction between spirituality and religiosity needs to be discussed given the confusion between the terms and also the strong repulsion or attraction that the mere word *religion* can evoke. Most importantly, the process of change into Spiritual Beings can occur within any religious organization or with no religious affiliation at all. Herein, religion is defined as belonging to a group that practices a set of beliefs, behaviors, values, and attitudes that are based on previously established religious doctrine and organized within an institution. The religious doctrine can be the Bible, the Koran, the Torah, or any other body of religious literature that is collectively shared and adhered to. Religiosity provides a sense of community, a sense of belonging, and supports groups of individuals that share the same beliefs, values, and morals.

Spirituality is the experience of a deep and profound relationship with a higher power or essence that occurs at the level of the individual. Spirituality includes a sense of meaning and purpose in life, a personal belief system and principles to live by. Transcendent beliefs and experiences can occur through an awareness of, and appreciation for, the vastness of the universe and recognition of a higher power. A relationship with one's inner self develops with a deep connection to this higher power, which results in an increased capacity to love. This expanded capacity to love eventually leads to behaviors that focus on the greater good for all living creatures and the universe. Therefore, spirituality within any religious doctrine can lead people to this transformational process since all religions have this truth at the core of their original teachings. The process of transformation to *Homo nuovo*, however, is not dependant on any religious doctrine or paradigm and in fact, can occur without any religious doctrine at all.

Spirituality, on the other hand, does not include a God that has been described by a religion or specific body of writing but rather, the concept of God or a higher power is an inner force, a calling, or even life itself. This is the great mysterious force that brings life with the first breath of a new baby and the mystery that expels life upon death. This force is a felt sense that is personal and private.

The process of communing and communicating with this life force or higher power can be called *prayer* and comes in the form of thinking, talking, connecting, or meditating with the great space inside the self. This can occur at any time and in any way such as gardening, listening to music, spending time with a pet, playing a sport, cooking, watching a sunset or beautiful vista; anything that connects the heart to this higher power or essence will be called prayer.

As the body and mind transform, the need to commune with the essence or higher power becomes greater because it brings a deep sense of peace. It may begin once a week or even less but always in a personal and private way; each and every person will know how to connect with the greater force of life by how it feels. A deep and loving connection occurs. Once this connection has been made then the motivation to connect with it often becomes easy. The tranquility and sense of grounding it brings enriches one's life in a natural way. It almost seems too simple to be true.

Homo nuovo is the term given to a group of people who know this truth and are themselves changing through a path or quest to understand why they are on this planet. They are trying to understand the purpose of life on Planet Earth and how they specifically fit into this process. They are moving toward an inner journey and sense that nothing outside of the self can provide permanent and long-lasting happiness but rather, happiness has to come from inside the self. This longing for something more than what exists in everyday physical life brings forth a quest that literally changes the mind and the body.

The changes that happen during this quest are part of a process of change that occurs on a continuum; at one end people are barely changing at all and are operating purely from their five senses. They believe the world is about material gain, competition, acquiring wealth, pain and suffering, joy and all things that can be seen, smelled, felt, tasted, and heard. The world at this end of the spectrum is only what you experience through these modalities.

At the opposite end of the spectrum is the Spiritual Being that has transformed beyond the five senses to what can be called *meta-sensory*. That is, a person who lives through more than five senses and develops skills and abilities beyond what the five senses alone can provide. These people also live with an incredible depth of love for all life, have a powerful personal connection to a higher being, a connection to all people and all things in the universe, and are able to manifest life experiences through thought and feeling alone. Every human is living somewhere between these extremes and is growing and changing at their own perfect pace. If the feeling is such that one is drawn or driven to consciously transform then the process will happen very quickly when that path is taken. Though there are many paths to becoming a Spiritual Being or *Homo nuovo*, the strategies in this book are just one path.

No matter what path is chosen, religious or spiritual, all paths will eventually lead to the same goal when a conscious choice toward spiritual transformation is made. When we accept life's hardships and trials as part of our life's path and part of our own growth, then eventually a blanket of peace will come over us. Life begins to feel right even though we know it may be difficult. Prolonged anxiety, fear, or unrest tell us we are not making the right choices and if, over time, these feelings do not abate, this may be a clear signal that something is amiss and that we need to listen to the anxiety or pain as a calling for change. When we are in the wrong job, with the wrong partner, or making a decision that goes against our own moral code, then the inner feeling is the guidance indicating that we do not want this in our lives. Suffering becomes a signal for change and an impetus for transforming.

As we listen to our inner feelings then the transformational process can begin and the time to connect to a deep and loving source within the self is taken. There are no rules for how to connect with this but the need for connection becomes greater and then transformation accelerates faster. Life becomes more peaceful, even in the face of difficult life circumstances, and by consciously connecting to a source greater than one's self, movement toward *Homo nuovo* begins.

CHAPTER 2

FROM THE BEGINNING

———

*This chapter is dedicated to
the many people over the years who believed
in me until I believed in myself.*

ASIDE FROM THE famous prophets such as Buddha, Moses, Jesus, and others over the course of human history, there have been countless individuals who have transformed into Spiritual Beings in some way. These have been normal individuals who originally had no special place in the world yet began to develop exceptional skills and a sense of being connected to all things in the cosmos. These people have come from all cultures and traditions, from the Aztecs, Maya, Inca, Navajo, and First Nations. They have been from the ancient civilizations of India, China, Greece, Rome, and Egypt. There are saints and holy men and women from all over the world who have transformed into Spiritual Beings at some or many levels. There is perhaps no culture or race that has not had individuals who have transcended existence as a five sensory human to experiencing life as metasensory humans, while transforming into *Homo nuovo*.

The First Peoples or indigenous people of the world lived in harmony with people, spirits, and nature while blending all three into one inseparable realm. The earth itself was an integral part of human existence as there was no boundary between the self and the earth so our planet and all its creatures were one family.

Communication between humans and the earth beyond the five senses has always been vital as special insights and gifts are received from these communications. The First Peoples of all nations have had chiefs, medicine men and women, and great seers who have lived with a deep sense of interconnectedness with all of creation. They have had a belief in equality for all life including plants and animals, bringing a respect to all of existence. They lived with a knowing for the long-term effects of the planet and the cosmos; understanding how the earth was a vital structure in the entire system of the universe, and what was required for her healthy existence. Life was lived with the continuation of life as a goal, rather than what is needed or wanted in the moment. The First Peoples on Planet Earth were perhaps laying the foundation for the transformation of humans, by understanding the intricate connection among all life.

In ancient Egypt the major concern was that of spiritual awakening where individuals could overcome ignorance and emerge out of the darkness into the light. In this era many people were taught to become healers while others were taught how to construct buildings with a harmonic resonance that spoke directly with its environment. It was understood that subtle energies could be felt and many were taught to change their bodies in order to amplify intuition. Teachers were those that had mastered the art of transformation and were then able to initiate others into becoming consciously aware that they were more than just the human physical body. The transformation of humans into Spiritual Beings was well rooted in this civilization.

Many traditions of spiritual development moved from Egypt to others parts of the world such as Greece, by showing up in the works of Pythagoras, Socrates, and Plato. Pythagoras is often referred to as the father of Western scientific tradition but was trained by Egyptian priests before he began teaching. It was said that he had rare visionary power and was in fact a shaman. He espoused the connection between all things such as music, numbers, and spiritual development. Pythagoras was able to understand the unconscious mind and the drive for some to have union with the divine. Socrates, another great philosopher, also spoke openly about his experiences between spirit and intellect. He was said to have precognitive perception and credited his thoughts to be from a channeled source. Socrates is often regarded as the wisest man who ever lived yet he attributed his wisdom to a source outside of himself that was obtained through extrasensory perception. A student of Socrates, Plato, compared the human condition to that of slaves in a cave, who can only see shadows of passing people and objects. The people in the cave eventually come to accept the shadows as reality rather than considering the source causing the shadows; he compared this to ignorance of the spiritual world. Plato, like Socrates and Pythagoras, espoused a reawakening to the eternal, spiritual existence humans have been experiencing for eons.

More recently, the Western world has been introduced to the wisdom of gurus, saints, and seekers from the Indian Tradition. This tradition consists of numerous individuals including Sri Aurobindo, Mother Meera, Maharishi Mahesh Yogi, and countless others who have been awakened to the transformation of *Homo nuovo*. Within their own tradition, they have come to know that they are connected to all of life and all of the cosmos. They live with a deep and profound love for all things and often have metasensory abilities that develop with devotional practice.

Throughout the past there have been numerous accounts of the spiritual transformation of humans but historically, this phenomenon had been permitted only by those of priestly or highly educated stature. In more recent times, people from all walks of life are able to explore spiritual transformation for themselves. What was once exclusively protected by mystery schools and cults of ancient times, or held sacred and secret, is now open for people to explore for their own development. Writings of all forms from popular culture to metaphysical to intellectual can be accessed for numerous others to explore. Movements, such as Indian mysticism and yoga, spreading around the world have helped people explore their own sense of spirit in the body. Metasensory abilities and perceptions are now popularized by mainstream television programs, books, and Internet information, making the process of transformation easily accessible to anyone interested in delving into this for themselves. The possibility for transforming spiritually has become widely available as it is no longer held secret for those only in positions of power, prestige, or influence. People from all walks of life began reading, meditating, discussing, and sharing the possibility of spiritual transformation. As practices spread and people shared what they learned with each other, the seeds of change were planted. The time has now come that those seeds have grown and the changes have occurred in large numbers; masses of people have transformed or are transforming on the planet, forming this new race of humans.

CHAPTER 3

THE CRISIS HITS HARD

———

*This chapter is dedicated to Cameron, who bought
me the first book that began the changes in me in
Ogunquit, Maine. He then, unknowingly to both of
us, started me on the path to transformation.*

EVERY SINGLE HUMAN being will come to face painful and difficult challenges in life. This is a universal reality of being human. It is the nature of life itself that brings forth situations that cause pain, hardship, and crises, which can occur at any age or stage in life. When difficult life challenges occur this is usually met with shock or intense emotional pain and the natural response is to resist both the wave of emotions that are elicited and the situation itself. Like a fast-moving train, the trials of life seem to come from nowhere or have been building for many years and finally come to a head.

The nature of these crises is vast and can include any life situation that adversely impacts one's personal life in a major way. These include various health issues, death and dying of loved ones, losing a job, witnessing a crime or catastrophic event, relationship issues such as separation or divorce, family turmoil, or financial crises at the personal, corporate, or global levels. People can be hit with one or more crisis at a time but the result is a shocking halt to one's normal life pattern. These events wake us up to the call that the life we have been living is not what we thought it was. It is also a call to look closely at how we are living and to question why we are living as we are. When someone is diagnosed with a life-threatening illness this can be the moment to wake up to one's own life and ask what needs to be done. Do relationships need to be mended? Do new modalities of healing need to be explored rather than simply accepting a one-venue form of healing? Does the illness carry a message and, if so, what could it be?

When a job is lost, perhaps this is the time to ask what the greater purpose of life is in terms of working and service to the planet. Rather than letting fear set it, perhaps looking at the situation as a point of freedom and an opportunity to make a more meaningful contribution through one's work can be explored. A new approach to the situation may bring a new and much needed change.

The initial response to any tumultuous change is to resist the change or the emotions that accompany it. People often deny that anything is actually happening such as refusing to accept a life-threatening diagnosis of a spouse or that a child has a serious mental disorder. These are difficult life challenges and often cannot be accepted or faced directly; however, the resistance itself causes tremendous pain. Facing the challenge is often not as painful as resisting it but resistance comes from fear of the unknown and fear of not knowing what to do.

The reality is that we change and grow from the pain when we allow it into our lives and permit it to do its work. The tendency is to numb out with drugs, alcohol, relationships, work, or any other distraction that will keep the situation at bay. These very difficult things actually allow us to stretch and grow when we have the courage to face them and be changed by them. By facing the fact that a loved one is dying we are able to expand our own capacity to love during that time. By facing the fact that a spouse is unfaithful we can then break our own patterns and move into a new relationship that allows greater growth and a life that could not be lived in the old way. By facing the reality and pain that a child has a mental disorder, we can then seek forms of treatment and learn a higher level of compassion. Facing the crises, in whatever form they may come, is the beginning of a life-changing process for the better.

The passage of time alone does not change us or teach us new ways of being but what we do in that time is what really matters. It seems that conflict and painful situations are pivotal for humans in terms of spiritual growth; allowing the pain to do its work is what sparks the light of change from which we can begin to grow and become something new. Resistance keeps us the same.

Accepting our crises as they appear and facing them with courage and openness creates the process that we can call the first step. To continue thinking in our old way creates blocks to new thoughts and feelings coming forth. Often the tendency is to keep doing what we do because that is what we know, which of course will only bring us the same results. When a partner continues to be unfaithful and we forgive and move on without any real emotional or psychological work then we continue to live in deceit and dishonesty. When we stay in a job of great dissatisfaction for the money alone then a deep sense of emotional emptiness will always be the result. Using drugs and alcohol to numb out a life we do not want keeps us living the life we do not want. It cannot be any other way until we choose to change our thoughts and feelings about a life situation in a profound way.

The crisis then is the starting gate to a new life. If it is received with courage, openness, and wonder then personal change can begin. With this, crises and pain eventually come to be seen as a great privilege. These are the gifts that initiate change because without crises, we rarely move to a new way of being. When new thoughts and feelings begin to stir then behaviors change in relation to the thoughts and feelings. Crises, though painful, can now be accepted as the wake-up call to change ourselves from the inside. It is from here that the world begins to change, not because it is different but because we are able to see, know, and feel it differently. We begin to see a world that is embedded in the world we see with our eyes but were unable to see it with our eyes alone. We begin to know the world in a rich and complicated way but we were unable to know this with our five senses alone; and finally, we begin to feel a world that we are embedded into where we are connected to all people, all life, and all of creation. As we move along the continuum of spiritual transformation our sense of being becomes richer and our lives become far more meaningful than ever before. It all begins with the conscious choice to do something different when facing pain.

CHAPTER 4

IRREVOCABLE CHANGES BEGIN

———

To my mother, Vincenza (age ninety),
who never ceases to transform.

WHEN THE BODY and the mind begin changing in relation to difficult and painful life situations, then everyday events can no longer
be tolerated as they once were. One noticeable change is often a
heightened sensitivity that develops in relation to many forms of
environmental stimulation. Sounds, smells, sights, tastes, and
physical sensations are all felt to a much higher degree. Due to this
heightened sensitivity the need for time in solitude or for peaceful
environments begins.

The inability to tolerate loud or chaotic environments is one
of the very first changes to develop. Violence or aggression on TV,
the Internet, from video gaming, in the home, or in society, becomes more difficult and painful to bear. What once was blocked or
numbed out of everyday awareness can no longer be numbed out or
tolerated because the sensations penetrate the body and the mind
in a very different way. It is as if the membrane between the body
and the outside world has been made thinner and now the effects
are so much stronger. Violence in any form is experienced through
the senses in a deep and profound way when previously this may
not have been noticed or acknowledged. The ability to deny this

realm of behavior is no longer possible and the reality of its existence becomes more and more clear.

Violence in the form of swearing, emotional outbursts, hitting,
raging, or whatever mode it may take is no longer tolerated. This
behavior hits the body and the emotions very hard, when once, not
so long ago, it went unnoticed or even accepted as the norm. It is
as if the senses are on a dial to regulate the amount of information
or sensations allowed into the body and now that dial has been
reset. If the senses were once allowing 30% of the information from
violence to be let in, they are now allowing 80% of the information
in. The effects from violence are so much greater and this does not
dissipate with time; if anything, sensitivity increases over time and a
heightening of awareness develops.

This new level of heightened awareness brings forth new
feelings toward what is occurring in one's own environment and
in the world in a new way. Numbing out the experience of mental
or emotional pain is itself an assault on the body and even the
slightest form of pain is felt very deeply. Pain becomes a signal
that something either inside the body, such as thoughts or feelings, or out in the environment, is having an impact. Gradually, a
sense of waking up to a new way of seeing, knowing, and feeling
the world occurs.

Another change that may develop is the sensitivity to certain
odors. Strong odors, especially those that are not naturally occurring in the environment, begin to affect the body in negative ways.
Nausea, headaches, and other deleterious effects begin to occur
from odors that the body does not want to experience. This sensitivity may increase over time and natural odors are the only ones that
the body can withstand.

Along with these changes may be a sensitivity to touch. Certain fabrics against the skin or harsh chemicals in contact with the skin, for example, may become intolerable. This is expected, for as the body's senses are changing and becoming heightened, they also need to be respected; gentle sensations are now recognized and desired. Slowly a sense of kindness toward the self becomes a new way of being.

Along with sensitivity to stimulation from the environment may come a deep feeling of emptiness. The behaviors and things that once filled the body with joy and contentment no longer seem to be having that effect. Filling one's life with material objects was once fulfilling but eventually, there is a keen awareness of an empty space on the inside. Once this comes to the forefront of consciousness, buying new things has a very short lifespan in terms of joy. Be it cars, clothes, or electronic devices, these do not fill the emptiness for very long. Eventually awareness arises that links the emptiness to something other than material things. Though material things are very nice and some pleasure is still had from them, the deep meaning they once held begins to dissipate.

Achievement striving, in terms of winning at sports, getting promotions at work, or being competitive in any way, may begin to lose its luster as well. The good feelings around winning or achieving are short lived and get shorter and shorter with time. It eventually becomes evident that the empty space cannot be fed from outside events no matter how valuable they are held by society.

Everyday activities such as playing sports, watching television shows, or even traveling also begin to prompt emptiness. Conversation about everyday events or popular culture cannot be engaged in for very long and a need for deep and meaningful conversations about life, death, the universe, science, spirituality, and other vast topics becomes evident. As conversations and connections to other people become stronger, there is simultaneously something missing in terms of a deep and meaningful connection to material things outside of the self.

One of the biggest changes to develop may come in terms of romantic relationships as they too take on a new meaning. The realization that finding a special someone to fill the empty space inside of the self will be a temporary solution becomes clear. A new partner, a new lover, is sadly not the answer to the emptiness. There is no one in the world that can fill the longing inside the self in a permanent way.

As the transformational process continues the world no longer feels like the same place it once was. There is a sense of waking up to something; perhaps something intangible at first until a new perception becomes the normal way of seeing, feeling, and knowing the world. There is a world embedded within the world, so to speak, which lies within the regular goings-on of working, playing sports, visiting with friends, and trying to make ends meet. There is a feeling that there is something more that may or may not yet be perceived but feels like a pulling or tugging from within the heart or the gut.

This pulling or tugging eventually leads to searching for some answers; to finding something to fulfill a curiosity because one begins to feel that something important is missing in life. What that something is, may still be unknown, but a need to find the missing piece begins. There is also a deep sense that there is no going back to what once was fulfilling as a solution, be it money, cars, relationships, travel, or promotions.

One way to embark on the search for answers is by reading material that introduces the topic of spirituality in some way either directly or indirectly. This can occur by seeking out spiritual books, literature, or popular novels. The awareness that this level of spiritual reality exists for many people in the world is revealed in books of many forms, and this reality that was once unseen begins to be recognized. It is as if books speak to the reader directly and reveal a level of spiritual connection that now resonates within. This can occur in a mystery novel as the author speaks of deeper life meaning through the plot and characters of the book. It can occur in a science fiction series, which reveals profound spiritual principles that can now be recognized. If unrecognized, the stories are enjoyable and entertaining and kept simply at that level until the awareness is ready to accept and see something more.

Books on art and science speak of a connection to all life in ways that are new and life-changing. The awareness that many people have known about a greater spiritual connection and the transformation of humans into Spiritual Beings is being communicated but more importantly, is now being understood, which then aids the process.

This level of spiritual connection slowly becomes evident in numerous forms of popular culture, which were once considered purely for entertainment. It becomes clear that the creators of movies are sharing a message of spiritual connection with the world. The message comes out in imagery, in dialogue, and at times is blatantly obvious to viewers yet goes unrecognized if the openness to the spiritual level of being has not yet begun. A movie made for entertainment purposes now awakens spiritual stirrings and affirms this realm of existence.

Art and music are perhaps among the most widely used venues for sharing spiritual messages and evolution. Sculptures and paintings reveal the message in profound ways. Again, if one is not open to the awareness of a spiritual realm then the art piece is simply a beautiful aesthetic expression reflecting something in the world. If one is open to the searching and stirrings of a spiritual self then the art piece becomes an object of loving connection. One can feel the artist's intentions and creation at an insightful level. Once the changes inside the self have begun, it becomes clear that the world has known about the spiritual realm within humans for eons, and it is now unraveling as we each participate in it for ourselves by letting it into our conscious awareness in many different ways.

Music of every form carries the message of spiritual connection into the world in an infinite number of ways. Musical lyrics clearly espouse the oneness of all things and the connection of love between all creatures. Music from rock to country to classical now takes on a new level of meaning that once went unnoticed. The message is everywhere and is now sparking the spiritual search and feeding it at the same time.

As exciting and stimulating as this new-found awareness is all around us, it can also be accompanied by a feeling of emptiness in environments that were so familiar. Those things that once felt good and fulfilling are now understimulating. The same old conversations about everyday things are meaningless now. The same places shared by people who do not have an inner spiritual search feel so empty now. There is a need to find something that fills the space inside the self that was once abated with material or emotional things, so a relationship with one's inner life begins to develop in a new way.

This relationship begins when one's inner world has been

activated and the changes within the self likely cannot be stopped. Though they can be temporarily halted, the search and inner tugging will not abate. The need to find long-lasting fulfillment and something that is permanent in one's life is strong. The need to find a spiritual solution is sensed as the way out of the emptiness. Another romantic relationship will not do. Buying more material things appears to be a temporary fix. Changing jobs or moving to yet another home result in the same empty feelings. Another hobby doesn't keep the excitement for long. The irrevocable changes have begun because the inner stirrings have triggered the evolutionary process at the spiritual level. Though everything is very different now and being in the world feels so very different, it may still look exactly the same. In reality, nothing is the same anymore.

CHAPTER 5

WHEN FOOD FIGHTS BACK

———

To Anna, Frank, Mario, Pino, and Mary who have
all taught me that food is a form of love.

SINCE FOOD IS the substance that literally becomes every cell of the body, one's relationship with food takes on a new meaning in the process of spiritual growth. Whatever foods are eaten become the organs, the hair, the nails, the blood, the skin, and every other possible element of the living human body that ingested it. Though people have generally come to be disconnected from their food, its importance has not changed. Food is still the stuff of which the body is made. Each component of a food is transformed into the body's needs so the body itself is merely a reflection of what is ingested. If foods full of nutritive substances and high energy are ingested then the result is a healthy and energetic body. Foods low in nutritive substances and energy-producing capacity produce a sluggish and unhealthy body. As the body changes with spiritual growth, then the relationship to the food that builds the body also changes and reflects the progress.

One change is that the body begins to have different needs in terms of what is ingested. The most obvious and startling example is that the body rejects certain foods by not being able to tolerate them, or, by having an allergic reaction to them. Foods that do not agree with the body's own balance are rejected, signaling that a change is wanted, and actually needed, at the physical level of existence.

Food sensitivities and allergies are on the vast increase globally, which is a sign that the relationship to one's food must be reconsidered. Food sensitivities indicate that the body does not want a particular substance and though small amounts may be tolerated, the body does not function well with this ingestion. Food allergies are an extreme case and a very loud signal that a food is so harmful that the body not only cannot tolerate it, it will die if this substance is ingested. The message here is clear: some foods have become an enemy to the very body they are trying to nourish. A change in eating habits is not only called for in these circumstances, but necessary for survival.

It seems that as the body is changing, it can no longer tolerate substances that are not in harmony with its own transformation. Some foods have become contaminated with toxic chemicals in the production process or from the environment itself, such as the soil or the sea. A reaction to these foods is an indicator that the body's needs are not being met when they are ingested; the body is calling for more care and balance. Foods that are contaminated with chemicals for the purpose of increasing shelf life or enhancing flavors are not natural to the body's own chemistry and, therefore, are not being tolerated by more and more people. The human body itself has a natural rhythm with the earth and the foods produced from it so the more we move away from this connection, the more the body seems to rebel.

Spiritual growth is aided by foods that are produced naturally and are part of the natural world such as organic fruit, grains, fish, vegetables, and meats. The closer these foods are to being naturally grown and produced, the better the body will respond to them. Foods that have been contaminated with chemicals in the production process and are then contaminated further with processing into convenience or high shelf-life foods will likely have long-term negative effects. The body will begin to store large amounts of fat and have other negative consequences from ingesting unnatural substances such as headaches, gastrointestinal problems, and joint pain.

It is a natural progression on the path of spiritual transformation that more natural foods are chosen and more care in eating eventually develops. This may occur gradually but in time, the changing body will seek out foods that assist its own advancement, and then this is translated into how one feels in terms of energy and well-being. Paying attention to the body's wisdom and what will nourish it properly becomes a normal practice.

As eating habits change to more uplifting and energy-producing foods then the way they are eaten also changes. Eating food on the run or in a car while rushing around is also no longer appealing. This form of sustenance is felt, at a deep level, to not be nourishing for the body as more self-care and self-concern is taken. Each body slowly discovers for itself what feels beneficial and what feels destructive because there is a direct relationship between what is eaten, how it is eaten, and how the body feels after ingesting particular foods.

Feeling ill, tired, sluggish, or heavy after eating certain foods is a signal to change food choices because the body wants vitality and wants to be well. Lethargy is not something that is welcomed now so conscious eating to keep the body's energy high becomes the normal custom. Spiritual progression now brings with it a need to care for one's self at the physical level in a way that once was perhaps unnoticed.

As transformation continues, choosing unnatural foods becomes unappetizing or intolerable for the body to ingest. Cravings for unnatural foods deceases and cravings for natural, fresh, and organically produced foods increases. The joy from enjoying the freshest and most natural foods abounds as the physical body feels better and better over time. Another change that naturally occurs in relation to food choices is the amount of food that is eaten. Eating portions that are larger than what the body naturally needs begins to dissipate as the body's own balance of food and energy becomes regulated. Skipping meals and not nourishing the body regularly throughout the day is also a behavior that shifts. Eating slowly and in the right proportion becomes part of one's spiritual practice and a heightened level of awareness develops around this ritual.

With heightened awareness comes the realization that food is no longer to be used as a form of entertainment or as a numbing substance for the emotions. As awareness of food and the manner in which it is ingested increases, then the relationship to how the body feels with certain foods increases, and naturally, the connection to one's emotional life is made. Food is not used as a drug to numb out emotional pain of any kind, including boredom. The body naturally ingests the amount of food it needs to feel well and emotions are dealt with directly, rather than indirectly. Becoming in tune with the natural balance of food and its relationship to one's overall well-being is an integral part of the spiritual process.

The view that foods low in nutritive value and energy-producing capacity are a "treat" also begins to change. Foods high in fat and sugar, while providing the body with no positive benefits, are slowly avoided. What changes is the attitude toward these foods as one is waking up to a new reality. Foods are now seen for what they are: a part of the living planet that, when ingested, become part of the living body. We literally ingest parts of the planet in order to become one with the planet in a synergistic way. We see that a vegetable is actually the soil it grows in, the rain that it absorbed, and the sunlight that fueled it with energy to grow. We are eating the soil and the sunlight in the form of a vegetable. If the energy in the vegetable is now destroyed by processing or it is contaminated with unnatural chemicals, then the body is not being nourished by the planet in the way it was meant to. There is now a disruption in the natural energetic cycle of life.

Food now becomes a sacred substance. It is not seen as a mere survival element but a substance of significant importance. One's daily life revolves around this nourishment in a revered way. Foods are chosen carefully and become paramount in one's daily life. Rushing to work and rushing to social events does not take precedence over nourishment. Eating foods that have not been prepared with care is no longer acceptable. Taking an interest in what is eaten, how it was grown or raised, and how it was prepared, is now considered before anything is consumed. This form of self-reflection becomes a natural and wanted practice.

In some cultures, it is customary that food is not prepared by anyone who is angry, depressed, or exuding negative emotion of any kind. It is believed that the food itself will absorb the emotion of the person who prepares it so only love and care are taken when handling food. When one becomes more aware of the entwined relationship among food, the planet, and spiritual growth then nourishment becomes a new adventure. Foods are chosen differently, the way they are prepared is now different, and the way they are eaten is different. We become aware of foods that are slammed onto a grill or thrown into a fryer for mass production. With awareness, each ingestion of food becomes a celebration of life itself, knowing that the life energy from the planet and the sun are infusing the body with this essence.

Another shift that gradually occurs is the appreciation for the people who raised, grew, and prepared a meal and its ingredients. One begins to look at each ingredient and appreciate the entire chain of people and events connected to its existence. When looking at an apple, for example, one can feel the connection to everything that brought it to this form. One can feel the heat of the sun as people planted and tended the trees. One can sense the warm rain falling onto the trees so it can be pulled up into each branch, leaf, and fruit. One can feel the hard work of picking the fruit from the farm and the exertion of bringing the fruit on wagons to warehouses where the fruit is handled further. The people who wash and pack each apple are appreciated and it is understood that the apple contains the energy and effort of everything that has come into contact with it. The apple then becomes a symbol for the connection between the sun, the earth, and all the people who are linked to it. All of this then literally becomes the person who ingests it. The connection is now made and it is understood that food is linked to the dynamics of the planet and the global community in countless ways.

CHAPTER 6

THE ENVIRONMENT BECOMES AN ENEMY

---

*To all the students and colleagues I have worked
with over the years that were instrumental
in my own personal transformation.*

AS SPIRITUAL TRANSFORMATION begins to take hold, tastes and food choices change, certain smells become intolerable, harsh or violent stimuli are avoided, and ordinary sounds become too loud to be tolerated. The sensation of touch also becomes overstimulating as the body becomes more and more sensitive, and in tune with the five senses. The environments that were once familiar are now uncomfortable in so many ways. This may be very subtle at first, registering a mild sensation of irritation or unease, but as the body changes, this discomfort increases and new environments are sought out; it is natural to begin choosing spaces that do not assault the senses in any way.

One of the earliest changes that seem to occur is that the need for watching certain television programs decreases. Television programs, especially those that cause a numbing response or dissociation to one's own life, are no longer needed or wanted. Programs that elicit any negative emotion or cause disruption to one's inner life are no longer comfortable and seem to be avoided. When a program elicits a negative emotional reaction there is certainly avoidance to that reaction, but more importantly, there is an awareness of what is happening inside the body as it reacts to something outside the body. The inner life is no longer ignored but is given recognition and respect. In terms of environmental triggers such as television, a move toward programming that is educational, calming, or uplifting slowly takes place. Television is no longer the mainstay of entertainment or the greatest form of distraction because the emotions need a new venue in which to grow and change in a progressive way.

Use of the Internet also changes with the changing senses. Information with violence is an assault on the body and its inner life, which becomes more and more intolerable. This form of assault can be from excessive news that focuses on negativity, seeking or distributing information that elicits negativity, or information that causes harm in any way. The tendency to avoid this information increases until eventually it is completely avoided. Information for the purpose of being uplifted and positive education is slowly the trend that occurs with spiritual growth. Sharing and seeking information becomes a need in a deep and kind way so information being communicated to the body from the external world provides vital signals that trigger responses either toward or away from certain environments.

Environments that have less chaos and more order also seem to be necessary as the body adjusts to changes. Homes with irregular schedules lend themselves to chaos, which does not foster healthy growth at the physical, mental, or emotional levels. As an extension to these, the process of spiritual transformation seems to require a home environment that is orderly, so that too naturally begins to fall into place. Spiritual and religious practices have known this for eons and have created temples and places of worship around schedules and routines. These include morning prayer, meals that are served with nutrition and regular routine in mind, sleep schedules that are in sync with the body's natural circadian rhythm, and time for solitude.

As changes continue to occur, the types of environments that also become more and more difficult to thrive in are those that are very loud or very bright with unnatural light. Spiritual development seems to seek out environments that are calmer and more peaceful. The need for quiet spaces, softer music, and sounds that do not assault the senses are gravitated toward.

Similarly, brightly lit environments with unnatural light seem to cause discomfort and are generally circumvented. A balance between environments with unnatural light and natural light needs to be sought for the body to feel healthy and energetic. Missing this balance will quickly be manifested as illness or discomfort, which seems to be restored by spending time outdoors in nature. A sluggishness that pulls the body's energy level down can become the norm if too much unnatural light and indoor living occurs. Often people become accustomed to going from home to cars and then from cars to indoor work environments. Leisure time is also spent indoors at restaurants, shopping centers, casinos, and other unnatural environments. The sluggishness that goes with this style of living becomes one's normal way of being, but can slowly be shifted as awareness and environments are changed.

The need for spending time in more natural environments also increases and the need for fresh air and sunshine draws people to this. The result is a renewed energy and a feeling of inner peace. Nature is a place of balance for the human body and it is greatly rebalanced by the natural energy of the earth. Getting outside and moving around in the outdoors becomes essential because of how quickly the body is restored to a better feeling place.

It is now known that spending time outdoors allows the body to resonate at the same frequency of the earth. In fact, it is best if the body can be in direct contact with the earth such as when walking barefoot. This direct contact allows the body to synchronize with the natural rhythm of the earth, a rhythm that has been set for the human body since the beginning of time. Setting one's body rhythm to the earth is actually essential for human beings to feel at their best. Most people, however, rarely spend time outside and it is even rarer for them to touch the earth directly. People tend to live their lives indoors, work indoors, and when outside, rarely make contact with the earth directly with their skin. Shoes and clothing keep a separation between the body and the vital structure it needs to have contact with. As transformation occurs beyond the five senses, more time outdoors becomes a requirement. Feeling the earth against the skin and having sunlight directly around one's body becomes essential.

Environments that contain high levels of electronic or wireless equipment can certainly have negative effects on the human body. Since humans are simply an electromagnetic field of energy themselves, high levels of external electromagnetic energy can disrupt the body's natural field. Disruption can occur by cell phone use, cordless phones, wireless Internet, Wi-Fi, or any other device that emits electromagnetic radiation. A growing number of people are finding that exposure to high levels of electromagnetic radiation induces clouding in the head or brain fog, numbness in the hands or feet, blurred vision, pain, disruption of balance, flulike symptoms (nausea, dizziness, headache), sleep disturbances, extreme fatigue, and confusion.

The solution to decreasing these symptoms is to reduce one's exposure to electromagnetic radiation, unless necessary, and to ground the body well. Grounding can be achieved by using grounding devices and by spending as much time outdoors as possible while directly touching the earth. Living a life in the most natural environment possible greatly aids in keeping the physical body well.

As conscious awareness awakens to the effects that environments have on the body and on one's emotional life, then there is a prodigious need to create environments that will reduce deleterious effects. Home life is made calmer and treated as a safe haven for everyone in it. The workplace environment has to be changed completely or in some way made more tolerable. Social circles naturally change as negative people and circumstances are slowly avoided. This process is best undertaken slowly to give the newly evolving self time to become comfortable in new spaces. The result from choosing new spaces in which to live and work is that a longer lasting feeling of betterment and an increased quality of life is experienced. These new environments also set the stage for development to occur in the inner landscape: the world of thoughts and feelings. This, in fact, is where crucial transformation will occur.

CHAPTER 7

EMOTIONAL ENERGY

To Erin S. and Emma F., for pointing me
in the right direction for this book.

AS ONE BEGINS to see the connection between the outer world and the inner world of thoughts and feelings, then one of the biggest changes to occur is the constant awareness of one's own emotions. There is a shift toward noticing what is happening inside the body throughout the day, especially in relation to what is triggering the emotions from the outer world. One may begin to feel and reflect on anger rising at a particular situation, which in the recent past was a feeling not noticed, but even considered to be a normal part of life and character. Now when anger rises, rather than letting it take hold and run rampant with one's life, there is an observing of the anger, how it moves through the body, and the event it is connected to. Perhaps the anger is a message to the self that there is something in the external world that is not wanted. The event may be that a person is behaving in a way that does not feel right, a situation is going in a direction that feels like an attack, or information is contradicting one's own truth. All of these emotional triggers can now be seen as a signal for awareness and, rather than reacting to them, just noticing them and allowing them to have a life until they settle down becomes a new option. This is what builds character and eventually what makes one's inner life strong. Living with the full range of emotions and yet not having them be in full control of life is a new way of being and eventually creates a new kind of human. This human is not driven by emotions but is living with a deep understanding and a connection to them. Since emotions cause a physiological reaction in the body, which affects every living cell chemically and hormonally, by changing our emotional reactions we literally change who we are. By changing negative emotions into neutral or positive ones, we begin changing on the inside; we feel ourselves toward a new way of being.

There is a realization that develops in relation to strong emotions such as anger, and with this comes the notion that it does not have to be fueled or fed with negativity or fighting. In fact, the anger needs be felt and then extinguished from inside of one's self by recognizing what it truly is. Walking away from negative discussions and allowing one's anger to settle down can be one way to evolve emotionally. Reframing the situation as one's own life lesson rather than finger-pointing and blaming will also result in positive transformation. When changes are made within one's own self by first feeling then transmuting or decreasing the intensity of negative emotions, then spiritual transformation slowly begins to carve a new life from the inside.

Once a relationship to one's own emotional life begins with a strong emotion such as anger, then transmuting and decreasing other negative feelings such as jealously or envy can also begin. These emotions may arise but these too cannot go unnoticed when one is aware of the rich inner life that is occurring. When a particular feeling arises there is a mental awareness of what the emotion is connected to. It is this connection that is one of the most important qualities of spiritual transformation. People can no longer have emotional reactions without realizing they are occurring within the body itself; they do not need to be controlled by these emotions anymore as observations of life on the inside develops. When a woman feels jealousy or envy for a coworker, for example, she can immediately make the connection to her own inner world. This connection can allow new awareness of the emotion, such as realizing her feelings toward another are actually a feeling being generated from inside herself and are not being put there by anyone else. From this point of awareness, conscious choices can be made. If the realization is that her coworker is believed to be more beautiful than she is, then perhaps the inner change needs to be more self-care and more self-love. Responsibility is then taken for one's own inner world of feelings and outer circumstances are taken as flags for awareness to develop one's own emotions through circumstances that they are connected to. With this, another level of spiritual change occurs in that life circumstances are seen as events for self-knowledge and self-change rather than events that are happening out in the world that are uncontrollable.

Sadness, fear, anxiety, and depression are yet other strong emotions that can carve spiritual transformation as well. These emotions, when felt at a deep level, carry energy of change that seems to come from the core of one's being. When these are allowed to be felt and to have their say, no matter what that is, then changes can occur at the spiritual level. Perhaps the depression comes from a longing for a creative outlet, or for changes in a life pattern that no longer serves a purpose. Feeling the feelings, listening to the message, allowing the message to be heard, and then acting upon it is perhaps the unfolding of the new self like a rose that slowly opens to its own beauty. The emotions act as the gauge to propel the blossoming changes to occur in new directions.

As the connection to the inner world becomes stronger, negativity in any form, including complaining or gossiping, becomes more and more intolerable in the spiritual process. The reason for this is that complaining or gossiping is now felt physically in the body with reverberations of negative emotions. Exposure to such environments is either avoided or at the very least minimized, in order to protect the body from its harmful effects. Again we are reminded to create environments that sustain the emergence of the Spiritual Being in any way possible, which includes providing a safe and healthy environment for the budding new emotions to grow.

A major shift that can also occur is that contact with people who are uplifted by other people's pain or demise becomes extremely harmful to one's emotional life. These people now have to be recognized and avoided because their shameful pleasure brings a wave of oppression that is even stronger than other forms of negativity. Again, the emotional compass acts as a signal for one to move away from this form of discomfort or to simply observe without reacting.

The focus inward toward the rich life of the emotions allows one to notice them and then either express them or consciously transmute them into a more positive or calmer pulsation within. One can become the observer of external circumstances that elicit negativity in any form and consciously try to be neutral in relation to them; to not judge the situations as good or bad but to merely let them be as they are. We cannot always understand the larger purpose of external situations but we can begin to take control of our own reactions to them so an emotional reaction does not reverberate in the body in a harmful way. The focus now is not on what is going on outside of the self but, rather, on what is occurring inside the self, and how this inner life can be transformed into calmness and inner peace.

As spiritual modifications continue, environments that also become intolerable are those where people are living with secrecy. Secrets, whatever their nature, cause a negative vibration to loom in the air in a very oppressive way. Environments that hold secrets exude deleterious effects on the body even if this is not completely understood. Secrecy brings with it a foreboding energy that can be felt as a heavy weight in the body and over time can even be expressed as physical illness. With spiritual transformation comes a movement toward creating environments that are uplifted with honesty and transparency. This may not occur immediately but in due course and with conscious awareness, healthier, transparent environments are created or chosen.

As the focus is now slowly shifting more and more inside the body to the emotions then instinctual emotional reactions can be eliminated, or at least decreased. If a feeling of sadness or loneliness occurs then this too can be observed and examined. The process of transmuting emotions from negative to positive or neutral becomes a more common response. Emotions are like sirens that go off to indicate when changes must be made on the inside. The inner life becomes the "real" life that is attended to as much as possible and the circumstances outside the self become less important. The need to numb the emotions or cover them up slowly dissipates as emotional strength is built from within. Emotional strength becomes the cornerstone of transformation. It is not to say that painful circumstances do not occur anymore because of course they do;

however, the inner strength to face them, to feel them, and to recognize them rather than reacting to them, is now the driving force.

As one begins to befriend and learn about the emotional life, then for some, it may have to be acknowledged that emotions are far too severe to be calmed or even to be felt for long periods of time. In these circumstances, the emotions are very deep and have likely been in existence from childhood. This could be a case of deep anger that rises up without warning and literally takes over one's body and mind. The anger is akin to a demon that torments the mind and makes the body act in ways that cannot be stopped. This type of emotional energy is incredibly forceful and can get out of control very quickly. Other emotions such as profound sadness or guilt can also take over the mind and the body rendering it immobilized. For others, thoughts that are extreme and tormenting cause profound emotional suffering, which cannot be stopped by one's own will. These extreme emotions can get entrenched within one's psyche and over a long period of time can become a part of the personality itself. They are emotions felt at a very severe level, are extreme, and can take over one's life almost to the point of possessing an individual.

In these cases, the actual personality is unrecognizable when the emotions take over; it is only with trained psychological or psychiatric assistance that these emotions can come to be understood and coped with. An individual cannot overcome these emotions alone and when it is recognized that the power of these emotions is far too strong for one's own will then professional help is the only answer for progression. There is a real emotional maturity that develops when one realizes that one's emotions cannot be self-managed and professional help is sought. With professional guidance, the layers of deep emotional pain can be realized, recognized, and transformed. A psychic shift is certainly possible.

For those who can consciously choose to stay calm and peaceful, either on their own or with professional help, then certain external circumstances are simply avoided or observed without judgement in order to live in peace. If the news on the television or in newspapers is too upsetting, for example, then reducing exposure to these is practiced. A healthy balance is sought with the emotions acting as the gauge for appropriate behavior.

Life events and interpersonal relationships that include game-playing, lying, stealing, deceit, or cheating also begin to change. As we observe ourselves participating in these behaviors we begin to realize that the emotional life attached to them is purely negative. These behaviors drive the negative emotions to a heightened level and become, in themselves, a means to an end. Lying, for example, brings with it a drama that creates more and more negativity; this vicious cycle of feeding the negative emotions with lying then becomes a way of life. Feeling bad on the inside becomes the old friend. Awareness is the new friend that can help one part with those old familiar feelings. With this level of transformation come relationships that are based on honesty and trust, which become more comfortable as one's emotional life becomes stronger and more satisfied with positive emotions. That is, feelings of love, joy, being uplifted, and happiness, and it is as though the body has become recalibrated for a new pulsation.

Once this recalibration occurs, another change that may occur is noticing that the presence of certain people can drain one's energy. These people seem to cause an overwhelming sense of exhaustion; it's as if all of one's own energy is being drawn out of the body. The body physically tires and the emotional reserves become completely depleted. One knows this has happened because the physical body looks very tired, the face becomes drawn, and it is all one can do to drag one's body away from the destructive source. The reason for this is that negative drama produces and expels large amounts of negative sensations that extend outward to others. Family members, friends, coworkers, and even strangers can absorb the negative vibrations emanating from certain individuals. In the process of spiritual change, we become more and more aware of people or circumstances and, more importantly, the negative ties that may bind us to them. The heavy emotional weight and the physical discomfort that comes with certain people become more and more obvious as emotional awareness develops. We no longer ignore the dark choking undercurrent emanating from someone who is smiling and saying all the right things but feels so off the mark to us. We can no longer tolerate the face of deceit and dishonesty disguised in human nicety. The emotional compass literally becomes the truth serum for all human interactions, no matter how pleasant or agreeable things may appear on the outside.

Another major shift in order to preserve one's own emotional wellness is to begin the practice of having integrity in what is said and in what is done. When there is an inconsistency here between words and action, a huge drain of one's own emotional energy occurs. Having to keep up a charade of saying one thing and doing another and keeping track of all that entanglement is equated with turmoil in the inner life. Turmoil is then perpetuated by any inconsistencies in our own behavior. The practice of going inward and watching the emotional landscape keeps the behavior in check, as immediate unrest is recognized. As a result, one spends less and less time feeling negative emotional states and more and more time in positive, joyful states. The behavior that stems from this, inevitably, is one with more integrity.

Another major change to eventually occur is to recognize behaviors that feel so very good at the time of engagement and then cause us to feel very bad after the fact. Such behaviors may bring feelings of joy or thrills but later they result in remorse, guilt, physical illness, pain, or sadness. If this is the case then one must come to recognize the cyclical pattern of the positive-to-negative emotion and eventually decide to not repeat it again. The cyclical pattern may be elicited from drug and alcohol use, sexual relations that do not have integrity, or any behavior that brings harm to others. As emotional maturity develops, one becomes more discerning with respect to the long-term effects of all behaviors and their connection to a healthy emotional life. Anything that moves the emotions away from joy, love, inner peace, and upliftment is, in reality, movement away from positive transformation.

CHAPTER 8

MENTAL MAKEUP

To Dermot M., who taught me the real meaning of Plato's
Allegory of the Cave. After we have seen the real world
we can no longer go back to the illusions that are cast.

AS SPIRITUAL EVOLUTION unfolds, part of the natural process is that each and every one of us begins to take responsibility for the very thoughts that we are thinking. The realization that thoughts are "things" and that they can be observed is revolutionary for the human mind. The simple act of noticing one's own thoughts is a big step toward transforming spiritually.

At times, thoughts seem to be constant, unrelenting, and even beyond one's control. Thoughts seem to have an entire life of their own but with awareness we can begin observing what is actually happening in the mind. Noticing how and when thoughts arise brings the realization that, at times, thoughts can be like a school of sharks, moving stealthily in the mind and suddenly attacking in frenzy. Before we know it, a story has been spun and has triggered a barrage of emotions deep inside the self. A story about the past comes back to life and gets bigger and bigger every time it is told. A story about a future that has not happened yet also gets spun in all directions; usually not for the better. Thinking about something long enough makes it feel as though it is actually happening in the body and the mind. In reality, we may be just sitting in a chair or driving along a highway while the mind takes over and goes wherever it wants to go while creating havoc.

When we observe people as they walk along streets or drive in their cars, they sometimes appear to be lost in their thoughts. They are far away in their minds, creating stories that are not about the life that is being lived in the very moment. The mind is running rampant with stories and scenarios of the past or the future, many of which never happened or will ever happen. The stories spin around and around running wild in many directions. It is a monumental step when the day arrives, if it has not already, when a person is no longer a slave to their thoughts but they begin participating in the process of reflexive consciousness, observing and realizing their own mind's creations.

This is the day when thoughts are noticed, which seems like a simple act, but in fact is incredibly transformative. By noticing one's own thoughts, there is a realization of how the mind works and where it will go if it is left unchecked. It will go to fearful places, it will create fictitious romantic affairs, it will see disaster everywhere, it will repeat the past over and over in great detail. It will create a life of its own, seemingly independent of the thinker.

When the light of revelation shines on these occurrences it is as if a hidden secret is finally revealed. Thoughts can be watched. Thoughts can be stopped. Thoughts can be changed. The constant stream of mental chatter no longer needs to run the show.

Once this pivotal revelation has been made, then just as external situations that produce negative emotions are avoided, thoughts connected to a long stream of similar negative thoughts are also avoided. We can actually choose to think without a barrage of thoughts taking over. We can say no to thoughts of the past that are so painful and as we slowly stop thinking them, they slowly fade away. As we observe them without participating in them, they diminish and as we observe them over and over again, they eventually cease to exist. We can say no to fictitious thoughts of the future and remain open to new possibilities rather than anticipating disaster.

As awareness of one's own thoughts becomes a common practice, the connection between those thoughts and the feelings they are connected to also grows. Situations that cause negative thoughts are diminished but, also, thoughts that cause negative emotions diminish. Often these thoughts are those that create drama inside the self by generating scenarios that elicit pain, fear, anxiety, depression, or any other familiar negative state. They are familiar because they have been felt and told over and over and over again by a mind that was not aware of what it was doing. A mind may repeat the story that it is never going to succeed, so it tells itself this over and over again with self-talk: "I can't do this," "I'm stupid," "He is better than me," "My parents didn't give me what I needed to succeed"; the stories are endless but at some point they do not need to exist anymore. It's a choice to repeat them or to extinguish them by not letting them have their say. The story is over when the thinker decides that it is over and no longer needs to repeat that story anymore. It's that simple.

Dramatic situations created in the mind can also give rise to stories that create negative feelings toward others as well. Stories come alive with transgressions that he said, she said, he did, she did. All of these stories create negative thoughts in the moment that are then carried forward for days and nights (even in sleep!). The stories become greater in the mind as they are told over and over again, which then changes the emotional life and, eventually, affects the outward behavior. The great revelation occurs when we realize that these stories do not need to cause pain again — ever again. Yes, they occurred, and yes, they caused tremendous pain, but they do not need to have power anymore.

People often feel that they need to hold on to actively thinking about negative things and by doing so, they can somehow change events. They can anticipate negative outcomes and somehow by thinking about them over and over again they will change the outcome for the better. However, thinking negative outcomes actually creates more negative outcomes. How can it be any other way? By practicing reflexive consciousness and watching one's own thoughts, the connection between negative thoughts of any kind and negative outcomes is made. Once this is realized, then the shift to changing old ruminative patterns arises. Again, we begin changing from inside ourselves.

One of the events that elicit great negative thoughts and feelings is that of watching or participating in negative news via the media or from others. It is with that, that we become cautious because thoughts are contagious. People often feel that they have to take in news from others because it keeps them informed; however, the manner in which it is delivered is often less informative and more emotion-provoking. Details are exaggerated and skewed to arouse pain, fear, anger, and all things harmful to the self. A common response is that people need to constantly listen or read the news so they can be prepared to act upon it. Writing strong, forceful letters in protest or telling others about the news they heard is going to somehow help change the world for the better. In reality, there is an addiction to the negative emotions that are created by negative news. The feelings that are triggered become old familiar feelings that have nothing to do with making the world a better place but have everything to do with repeating old thoughts and feelings in unconscious ways. In reality, we can make positive change in the world by being the change, not by reacting to it. Again, the practice of watching one's own thoughts and their connection to feeling is the beginning of being that change.

Once thought-watching begins, one of the repeated patterns that seem to arise is that of noticing judgment. Personal thoughts want to attack, criticize, point out errors, compare, and do all the things that can elevate the self while diminishing others. Of course it can go in the opposite direction as well where thoughts to elevate others and diminish the self can occur. This epidemic mental practice can get entrenched at an early age. It seems to be a chronic negative pattern that feeds chronic negative emotions such as shame, greed, and fear. Awareness of this mental storm brings about a practice of nonjudgment toward the self and others. Surprisingly, judgment has likely been occurring in the mind at many, many levels, including culture, race, gender, education, socioeconomic status, and the many other myriad of differences that one wants to perceive. I am better than you because I am more educated. You are better than me because you have more money. I am better than you because my culture is more prestigious. You are better than me because of the neighborhood you live in. The stories of comparison are endless and in fact needless. They are simply stories that spin on and on without end and without conclusion. It is by recognizing them as such that they can slowly be stopped. The chronic mental practice of judging and comparing can dissipate, which brings the realization that a more peaceful and pleasing emotional life results. By seeing and stopping the judgment we are elevating our quality of life from inside the self at the very core of being.

Once thought-watching and thought-changing begins to move in a more positive direction, the almost unbelievable realization occurs that what you think about repeatedly shows up in your physical world. Physical reality is actually created by thoughts and the feelings they are strongly connected to. Though many people may have heard this before, it becomes very apparent when one connects thoughts and events in the outside world in a meaningful way. Thinking about a friend with strong emotion will evoke a phone call or a random run-in at the grocery store. Thinking about anger and hatred toward a certain race brings a person of that race directly into a life situation. Thinking about illness in a deep and worrisome way is connected to a sore throat and cough a few days later. It is only by watching one's thoughts that the connection can be made that having the same thought repeatedly creates that very object of attention to appear in physical form. The way this occurs is now being understood across the planet by millions of people.

Firstly, it is recognized that every human being is a tuning fork, a vibratory field of thoughts and feelings that attracts to themselves what they think about and what they feel in a consistent way. If someone feels jealousy toward others then that person will literally vibrate with jealousy and attract this very thing into physical life. People with more material things, couples who appear happier, people with better jobs and more prestige — all will show up time and time again, literally answering the call that the pulsation of jealousy puts out. Physical reality is brought forth to the "thinker and feeler" so by thinking and feeling jealousy, this is exactly what is brought forth. It is not the case that one can create for someone else but, rather, the mind and emotions are the "self-generating force" of physical life.

Groups of people having the same negative thoughts and

feelings about other people draw that negativity directly into their lives. Group thinking and feeling about illness creates illness. Negative thoughts about relationships by the masses create tumultuous relationships. The pulse of physical creativity on the earth is that of thought coupled with emotion; any physical world situation or event is being created either by one person or a number of people in order for it to be so.

The next big step in spiritual evolution is to then reflect on how one is participating in the world with personal thoughts and feelings. Am I angry and therefore attracting anger and creating anger in my workplace and with my family? Am I judging people all the time and therefore creating scenarios of imbalance amongst people? Am I fearful of lack of money and therefore drawing myself to scarcity? When the awareness occurs that thoughts are things that create physical reality, thoughts are not left to their own devices. We also begin to reflect on what we are adding to the flow of creation with others since our thoughts add to the mass consciousness for all of humanity. Our contribution to the thoughts of humanity become carefully chosen.

A natural extension of this awareness is to then begin decreasing the mental chatter that gets out of control. The power in mental stories is realized and by repeating them over and over again, the strength of attraction increases. The mental landscape of thoughts is now watched but also protected, as if it were a newborn baby. It is not allowed to venture out anywhere it wishes. The mind is treated with reverence and is cared for, and nurtured; it is watched and guided and directed. This is the new life emerging in the mind of each and every human on earth.

CHAPTER 9

MAKING A CONNECTION

———

To my soul-sister Mirella S., for sharing
the path of Oneness with me.

ONCE THE SHIFT occurs toward spiritual transformation then a wonderful realization unfolds; that is, that there are countless others who are also on this path. We begin to recognize the transformation in other people by the way they speak and act, which is often revealed in the smallest of gestures. We may see a man in the grocery store who is patient and kind with an elderly customer in a way that we have never noticed before. We may see a woman at the workplace who will not participate in gossip but, rather, observes quietly and does not feed it with her energy. In another instance, there is the recognition of something different when a stranger in a crowded restaurant offers a table and chairs to a couple as he is leaving, in a most kind and loving manner. We begin to see, know, and feel a world within the world that was once out of our awareness because when thoughts change, then a different world becomes available. Not only do we see a difference in the world but there is also a stirring to participate in it and perhaps understand it.

The changes may also bring about a need to seek out others who want to connect and discuss spiritual matters in a deep and profound way. The shifts that occur in the mind and the body become a force of attraction but also a tie that bonds us to others who are similar. The quality of relating to others also changes so it becomes about caring at a deep level. It becomes about helping others, giving of the self, making positive changes, and less about what is wrong with the world. The connection to others slowly moves away from gossip, complaining, or focusing on one's own life conditions.

In many instances, people begin charitable work but caution must be given that it is not undertaken in a self-serving way: to impress others, to get a promotion at work, or to make one's self look "better" than others who do not participate in charity. As spiritual changes occur, charitable work shifts in the mind so the attitude becomes more about others as part of the self. Caring about others becomes about connecting with an open heart and, eventually, the sense of self dissolves, leaving only a sense of connecting. The gain is the connectedness itself.

Another great insight is that every person who comes into one's life, no matter how minimal the interaction, is there for a reason because they have attracted each other for a reason. There is something important to learn or to share with each other, and this is part of the grand design of life. Each of us is part of a complex and integrated system where we attract to us exactly what we need and the people we attract are perfectly in tune with those needs. Holding this in the forefront of the mind means that there are no bad bosses, no bad friends, no bad spouses or lovers, no betrayal, and no need for resentment in relationships. There is only learning so the deepest level of growth can occur. We can stop seeing differences in culture, skin color, race, age; all the things that are used to separate ourselves from each other which are usually rooted in fear. Fear that someone will have more resources, more money, or a job we may want. This thought pattern is usually learned at a young age, which teaches us to separate ourselves from others and keep others at bay. This is simply a thought and, when challenged, can be replaced with a new thought that is not fed from fear.

As a deeper sense of connection develops then the need for recognition also decreases. We do not need to tell people what we have, what we have done, or to be set apart from others with praise. We do not need to self-promote in any way, either directly or by putting others beneath us in some fashion. In fact, it becomes clear that all achievements in life are connected to countless people and when a success happens, it's because many people have made a contribution to that success.

If the CEO of a company donates a large sum of money to a charity it's because someone hired him at a job that paid him a very good salary. The salary could be paid because the company produced a product or service, which likely involved the efforts of many people who in turn each helped to produce the generous salary. This includes the people who work at producing the product one step at a time, people who answer phones, keep track of accounts, speak to customers, relay information to others in the company, and on and on it goes. The donation to charity carries the energy of each and every person involved.

Similarly, a doctor can help treat illness because she had people who gave her the opportunity to attend medical school, had very good teachers who gave of their time and skills; then there are the numerous individuals who built hospitals, clinics, medications, equipment, and all things that support the practice of medicine. A doctor does not exist as such alone. The connection to people is infinite and once this is realized, we can see that the boundary between the self and others really only exists in the mind.

As we expand our spiritual awareness and our consciousness then we also come to see the domino effect of our thoughts, feelings, and behaviors. What we do affects everyone around us and spreads like one domino hitting another, perhaps farther than we can even imagine. When a parent is verbally harsh or condescending to a child then the negative influence of that is carried with the child out into the world. That child then goes to school with the reverberations of those thoughts and feelings, and may act that out by hitting or name-calling other children. The recipient of that negative behavior then carries this home and acts out the pain with siblings by hitting, belittling, or name-calling. The original negative thought planted by a parent into one child continues to spread out to more and more people, which will eventually become rooted in the minds of entire neighborhoods or communities as that child grows into an adult with those thoughts.

The original form of negative thoughts and feelings can also be subtle such as using damaging words or constantly correcting someone, and thus reminding him that he can do nothing right. It can also be passive-aggressive by purposely not helping someone in order to let him struggle, or withdrawing support in some way so he can suffer. Negative thoughts and the pain they cause are all the same in the end, no matter what form they initially take. Every act that hurts others spreads like a cancer in ways far greater than people can even imagine when they are not aware of what every human act does to the planet as a whole.

The other side to this notion is that all positive thoughts, feelings, and behaviors also spread through a family or community like wildfire. When a woman helps one person in an unexpected way then that person carries an uplifted feeling, which can spread to others. When a man helps a stranger get gasoline for his stranded car then the recipient carries with him a little bit of upliftment when he carries on with his own life. Perhaps he tells the story to others and that uplifts them, too. In turn, they feel just a little better for having heard about the deed and they bring that home to their family and friends. When there is recognition of how far-reaching every single word or act spreads to others, then there is the realization that when one person acts with a positive word, emotion, or behavior then the whole world gets a little better too. Every thought, feeling, and action matters on a global scale.

Once we begin to accept our own part in the domino effect of the planet and take responsibility for what is in the mind and the emotions, then a new awareness of what we do means we attract a different life. Everything begins to feel right as we see the world in a different way. We realize that we are connected to all people and all things and that each and every one of us is part of the grand design of the world; we are no longer independent people fighting for recognition and survival. We are so much greater than that.

= CHAPTER 10 =

RELATIONSHIPS AND THE PEOPLE WHO POP UP

To my father, Eugene, for the inspiration
and guidance he gives me.

AS WE ATTRACT people to us by being aware that we are participating in who shows up in our lives we are also aware that it is these people who teach us to grow and evolve. Life is not coming "at" us but, rather, we are participating in it with our thoughts and feelings. We may find this hard to believe because people may not always be kind or friendly — in fact they can be incredibly mean-spirited — but nonetheless, these people become very important to us as we have attracted them to ourselves for a reason. People can act as a mirror for what needs to be seen or learned and often it is the most difficult or challenging people that can be paramount in terms of our own positive growth. Conversely, we may attract people who have the opposite tendency of the very character trait we need to learn and we fit each other perfectly, like a lock and key. A woman who needs to learn to not be victimized will attract aggressors over and over again until she overcomes victimization by self-empowerment.

People who are difficult and challenging can teach us new skills in terms of emotional regulation and control. When we are not yet trained in keeping unleashed anger in check, with either overt or covert anger, then angry people show up to show us that we still have a ways to go. On the other hand, perhaps we do not speak up when we need to and we bury our own needs in order to please other people. If this happens over a long period of time then anger eventually rises to the surface because it is a voice that is finally saying no, I do not want this in my life any longer. Either way, anger in relationships is the device that allows for personal growth to happen should it be recognized as such.

If we carry fear, jealousy, or envy inside ourselves then daily life situations will reveal themselves that trigger these. People will show up to present opportunities for us to see and experience our own emotions, especially if we are unaware of them. If we see this as an opening for something new, we can acknowledge the emotions and even find the root that likely began in early childhood. When this is acknowledged and dealt with appropriately the emotions dissolve and relationships that carry this lesson will also dissolve.

As our own mental and emotional lives improve then it can get more and more difficult to be around other people who are still not yet on the path as we know it. Being in a place where we see a woman lying to her husband can become difficult. Seeing a woman who is full of hatred and jealousy to everyone around her but interacts with a sweet, inauthentic smile can feel painful. Knowing a family member is lying to protect her sister's dishonesty or watching a young man deceive and manipulate people to get money from others become instances that are obvious and now clear. People continue to play their games of survival and ego fulfillment but when we look at this behavior from the perspective of opportunities for growth and development, we can understand this for what it is and stay detached. All of these seemingly negative interactions are there for people to have opportunities to transform spiritually and they may or may not know this. Even in extreme relationships that involve abuse, the abuser certainly has a lesson to learn but the victim too has to learn not be victimized ever again. It is only when enough pain and suffering from these situations occurs that change can happen. When we ourselves have transformed enough to no longer participate in these types of relationships, we can observe without judgment, slowly back away, and focus on our own positive growth.

When we begin removing ourselves as best we can from negative interactions we do so with deep love and with an understanding that everyone has their own lessons; we for them and them for us. Rather than becoming emotionally involved we observe and move past this to a more evolved state of being that sees new meaning in all relationships.

Interestingly, as we move away from people who continue to play out hatred, manipulation, possessiveness, fear, and other forms of negativity, we can open ourselves to people who have a much wider concept of love. Often people can only love a few others, and even then, only those in their close inner circle. They can love spouses, children, and perhaps a few family members. Friends may fit into the circle but they generally do not hold the same value as close family. Love is often seen as something someone else has, that needs to be received, and in return, love is given back in equal measure. The belief is often held that if I give love away then the cup is now empty unless someone else fills it up. In extreme cases, people feel completely empty of love and they try to desperately find others to fill them up. The truth remains that love comes from within us and not from others. It is a deep emotion inside every single person and it needs to be accessed from within. When we finally learn to tap into the love inside ourselves then we will feel fulfilled, and not until then.

Once we access the source of love from within then we open our hearts and our minds to a greater idea of what love can look like; we see that there is a much wider sphere of people to extend love to. There is no limit on how many people we can love. If we can try to live with this notion, even for a short time, we see that the more people we extend our own source of love to, the more love comes back to us, and the more loving we become. This is a never-ending cycle that feeds back onto itself resulting in a pulsating force that enriches our lives beyond anything we could have imagined. The original source, however, is always from within and not from anyone else.

Often people reject this notion of love because they feel it means there will be less love for that "special" person or persons. For example, I cannot love my stepchildren because that would mean less love for my own. I cannot love my friend because there would be less love for my spouse. This is a stingy possessiveness that in fact blocks the cycle of love back into our own lives. Love is a resource that was meant to be shared and it is only by finding it within the self and then sharing it that its abundance can increase.

We come to understand our relationships as a source of learning, personal growth, and a way to extend our love, which creates an endless well that gets filled by giving it away. This, however, must not be confused with attachment. Attachment in human relationships elicits fear and anxiety. There is also a neurotic imbalance that comes when the relationship is not based on pouring forth love alone. Fear that the person may die or leave. Fear that love will not be returned. Anxiety arises at the thought of not possessing the other. When the realization is made that this is not love but some distorted emotion, then there is a change from the old "I need you to complete me" to a kinder, more stable relationship. The new relationship holds an understanding that each is on a path to spiritual transformation and that must be respected, no matter how much our small, possessive form of love wants to hold on. When we allow ourselves to expand and grow then addiction to romantic relationships ceases; no more reaching outside of the self to other people for love or security. Love comes from within and then it is extended out. It is not the other way around.

Ultimately, we stop the cycle of pain and bliss and we replace it with a fundamental feeling of oneness. We no longer reach for love from others but, rather, it comes from 'a deep space inside the self and brings with it spontaneous rushes of joy and awe. Relationships become opportunities to expand ourselves out exponentially and to reach out as far as we can. We do this because we see, know, and feel the benefits coming right back to the source from which it started. That would be us.

CHAPTER 11

IT'S JUST A DREAM

To Marlene S., Rita D., Maria G., Nicolle M., Ally D.,
and Diane S.: the women who share my dreams.

FROM THE EARLIEST of times humans have known that dreams contain important information for the dreamer's waking life. Dreams have been painted on cave walls, written on stone tablets, told over and over in folklore, and play major roles in most religious texts. These nighttime images are known to act as a guide to thoughts, feelings, and waking day actions. They are a roadmap for waking life and provide both guidance and counseling for those who are open to them. As spiritual transformation progresses the meaning found in one's own dreams can become a rich source of information.

Dream images are very personal and they conjure up stories and scenes that are written in the context of the dreamer's own personality and paradigm. If a dreamer lives a chaotic life full of emotional turmoil, then dream stories and images will come in that chaotic form. The dreamer will find himself in strange places, with scenes changing constantly and emotions riveting. If a dreamer lives a life of deceit and dishonesty then dream scenes will reflect information that is played out in scenes of this nature. This dreamer may find himself involved in scenes with great violence, war, or crime being the main focus. Nonetheless, no matter what form the images take, the purpose of dreams is to help the dreamer see what needs to be changed or attended to in waking life.

If a dreamer attends to dreams by writing them down, paying attention to them, and trying to make waking day connections to them, then dreams will often speak directly to the dreamer. When dreams have been ignored or neglected then they may not be remembered or come in vague images that do not make much sense. The more they are focused on, the clearer they become in their content, and the more directly they will speak to the dreamer. If we ignore our dreams then they in turn will ignore us.

Dreams will always indicate waking life circumstances, whether they are occurring consciously or unconsciously. They provide vision into family dynamics, employment situations, financial concerns, or any of the various trepidations people have in their waking life. Generally, what people think about, feel, or do in waking life carries on into their dreams in a continuous manner. The information is in fact so vast that it will provide the dreamer with valuable insights at all levels of being: physical, mental, emotional, and spiritual.

At the physical level, one way dreams provide insight is that they will alert the dreamer if health issues are a concern. Forewarning dreams can occur for an illness long before the first symptoms are felt or even known to exist in the body. If health-warning dreams do occur, this is a sign to become conscious of the problem and to seek out possible early treatment. If, on the other hand, health-compromising behaviors are engaged in such as smoking, excessive use of alcohol or illicit drugs, extreme exercise, or under- or overeating, then these too will show up in dreams as a warning. Dream imagery will reveal any physical problem and its consequences for which the purpose is to protect the body from danger.

If the mind is preoccupied with constant worry and negative thoughts then these too will reveal themselves in dreams. These will show the dreamer that rumination is not a healthy or wanted practice; solutions to the issues may also be made known. For example, if a man is constantly worrying about his grown son who refuses to seek medical attention for an illness, then the man may be shown in a dream that avoidance of the doctor's office is a very important path of learning for his son. The man may also be shown that he is to let his son make his own choices and focus on his own life lessons and growth. Dreams tend to focus on the most current issue of importance in one's waking life so when they appear, this is the facet of life that should be given attention.

One of the most central features to dream generation is that of the emotional energy of the dreamer. Dreams are imbued with the active emotions of the dreamer in waking life, which then continue to be vigorous in sleep. Dream emotions can be used as a guide to become aware of one's emotions while awake. The tendency for people who do not pay attention to their dreams is to view dreams and dream emotions as entities separate from their own lives. Dream emotions do in fact reflect the dreamer's inner life and they tend to be the most important waking-day emotion at the time of the dream. Once this connection is made, dream emotions become a signal for something important that needs attention in waking day.

Similarly, one's own thoughts are clearly reflected in dreams, though many people disconnect this from their own waking life. Thoughts from waking day continue on into dream generation since the mind and brain do not stop functioning due to sleep. In fact, the dreaming mind looks very similar to the waking mind when measured in a scientific lab. The brain and mind are extremely productive during sleep, producing personal information for the dreamer, if she cares to receive it upon waking.

Finally, at the spiritual level, dreams are one of the greatest sources of insight. They provide information about the dreamer and how life lessons can be learned from everyday situations. New solutions to life problems, in a larger context, will also be offered in dreams. One's purpose in life can be revealed as well as paths as to how it can unfold in the realms of work, family, or others.

A helpful practice to explore transformation at all levels of being is that of dream interpretation. This is the process of taking the imagery remembered in dreams and connecting them in a meaningful way to waking-day situations. A woman may dream that she goes into her closet and finds two pigs' heads on the floor of the closet. With dream interpretation she discovers that she herself is "too pig-headed" and needs to look at this part of herself since it is causing numerous relationship problems. Another woman with breast cancer dreams of a black tarantula clinging to her breast and digging its claws into her. With dream interpretation she comes to realize that her cancer will slowly kill her if she does not take the treatment she initially rejected.

Dream interpretation methods vary greatly from therapist-guided techniques to self-guided methods. Perhaps the most important aspect of dream interpretation is to choose the method that works best and resonates true. If rich and helpful information is gleaned from a particular method then that is the one that should be used. Only by exploring many different forms of dream therapy can we really know what works for us and what does not. Additionally, dreams tend to have many, many layers of meaning and will provide information for waking-day issues in a composite manner. Interpreting a dream with one technique may reveal one level of meaning, which may be, for example, at the physical level. A dream may provide information that the body is being injured in a particular work environment. A second interpretation method may validate this information but provide insight into the fact that the work environment is linked to financial fears and irrational beliefs of scarcity. A third method may unravel childhood situations that began the beliefs around money and the attachment to fear. The dreaming mind will continue to provide information in a multitude of layers, if we are willing to delve into them. At a still deeper level, when exploring our dreams we may come to see that some are actually foretelling events about the future. *Precognitive dreaming* provides information and signposts about future events in great detail. Though often coined paranormal dreaming, a closer look at these images from people's dreams all around the world reveals that they are quite normal and very common. Most people have dreams about future events quite often and when they are ignored, they go unnoticed. This does not, however, negate the fact that they are occurring.

Precognitive dreams tend to be short, very vivid, and the last dream just before waking. People report more of these dreams as they consciously participate in their own spiritual transformation. Guidance is given during sleep to aid in all aspects of waking life as a step-by-step guide to choosing a mate, finding a career path, travel, relationships, health, and all other important life matters. For example, precognitive dreams will reveal the ultimate romantic partner in terms of happiness and self-growth and also provide warnings. Upon meeting a new potential partner a woman may have a series of dreams that he hands her a beautifully wrapped gift only to find the box is empty. This imagery may be cautioning her to assess this relationship in her waking day.

A precognitive dream may also provide a warning that a prospective job is not one for the path of higher learning and progress but merely for financial gain in a manner of greed. The dream imagery may be that a man finds himself in a new workplace environment and his desk is full of money. As he puts his hands in the desk drawer to take some of the money, poisonous snakes and insects come out from under the dollar bills to bite him. The dreaming mind warns the conscious mind of choices that are not for one's betterment; whether the warning is heeded, is up to the dreamer. The purpose of these dreams is to help people circumvent life challenges and accelerate growth with less effort and time spent on decisions that are not for one's ultimate upliftment. They also provide options that will decrease pain and suffering by averting paths that will ultimately lead to learning in this way.

Finally, many people in transformation report having *lucid dreams*. During these, we can become aware in the dream that we are actually dreaming. This state of dreaming is similar to spiritual transformation in that they both involve a form of waking up to something new that is in the current environment. In lucid dreaming we wake up, so to speak, and realize we are in a dreaming landscape. In this state, the dreamer can begin to solve waking-day problems such as finding treatments and cures for an illness or create works of art. New experiences can also be had during lucid dreaming that cannot necessarily be experienced in waking day.

Similar to lucid dreaming, spiritual transformation involves waking up and realizing we are living in a world within the world. This is one that was there all along though we did not know it. In both cases, the mind is fully focused but with a new awareness. This awareness can become the gateway to freedom as we awaken to the possibilities that lie in the very world we are just now coming to know.

CHAPTER 12

LIFE BEYOND
THE FIVE SENSES

———

To Linda O., for opening my eyes,
my heart, and my mind.

FOR MANY PEOPLE on the continuum of transformation, perception beyond the five senses begins to develop. Some people can hear sounds that others do not hear. Some see things others do not see. Still others develop sensitivity to sensations that cannot be described by the five senses alone. One person may see auras around people, plants, and animals. Others may know intuitively what will happen in the near future. Life in what appears to be the "normal" world begins to be more complex and enriching than ever before.

Clairsentience, or the ability to feel other people's feelings, may be one manner in which people begin to change. It is not uncommon to begin feeling anger, pain, attraction, excitement, or any range of emotion emanating from another person. This initially can be confusing since we may not distinguish between what is being generated from one's own emotional life or that of another. Over time, as the ability matures, it becomes clear as to which emotions belong to whom. The emotions will have a different quality when they are emanating from another person and discernment slowly develops with practice.

In terms of clairsentience, there is a blurring of the boundary between the self and others, so when we experience feeling other people's feelings, there is initially a sense about them that is not quite tangible. These sensations can occur as subtle feelings: someone who does not have integrity, a physical attraction that is felt but not seen in any way, or anger that permeates in and around an individual. As time goes on, the sensations occur with more and more frequency. Having a feeling that someone at work is lying and cheating, in order to get ahead. Knowing that someone is physically attracted to a married man and unconsciously changing her behavior in certain ways. All of these feelings and knowings will eventually be understood and managed. These feelings are not occurring so we can criticize or judge the people that are having them. They manifest so we ourselves can learn how to develop our new sensory skills and how to work with them within ourselves. The transformational process at this and all levels is about our own inner journey and development.

Some people may call their inner stirrings and new form of information *intuition*. This is the ability to understand something immediately with no effort or conscious reasoning. It is a form of knowing that occurs more and more as transformation progresses. Intuition is a very individual experience and develops uniquely in each and every person. Once it is recognized that perception occurs beyond the five senses alone and that this new dimension is emerging, then awareness of this ability brings it to the forefront. Similar to dreams, by focusing on this dimension the sensory skill is allowed to find its way into the world. As it is slowly trusted over time, it will get louder. As it becomes louder, further skills and perceptions with reveal themselves. This is one of the grandest features of *Homo nuovo*: that the world within the world is revealed through extrasensory perception and the more we participate in it, the more it will reveal itself to us.

We will know that we are participating in our own path of spiritual growth when *synchronicity* and signs in the physical world become commonplace. Synchronicity is when we experience events that are apparently unrelated, but actually occur together in a meaningful manner. One illustration: a man drives his car while thinking about his daughter and a truck immediately passes him bearing a logo that includes the company name — which happens to be his daughter's name. In another instance, a woman is trying to find a person to help her with her garden then immediately goes to a social event and meets a person who is looking for work as a skilled gardener. It is as if the universe is conspiring to aid and assist with every thought. It is listening and responding in numerous ways and there is a communion with a force that is alive and present for each and every one of us. We become aware of this force and begin to notice it and participate with it. Again, as we slowly come to trust these signs, they become more frequent until we are living in a transformed world where nearly everything is speaking to us with guidance and direction.

Of course, dreams, intuition, synchronicity, and all other forms of information begin to work together to provide an entangled form of guidance and insight to life's path. A woman, for example, dreams that she meets her life partner at a symphony concert and she knows him in the dream because of his deep, blue eyes. She in fact goes to a symphony one week later and is approached by a man with these same deep, blue eyes. As he approaches her, she glances at an advertisement behind him and she can just see only one word from the ad since he is blocking the full view. The only word she can see over his head is the word "yes." At that moment she gets a feeling deep inside herself that she should pay attention to this moment. Of course when the information comes to us, we must also test it by how events play out in physical reality. We still use our good judgment and good senses but we are now aware and open that there is much more going on than what appears directly in front of us.

A big change that often occurs as we transform is questioning our physical reality and developing a curiosity about death and the process of death. Many people live most of their lives never asking questions about where they were before they inhabited their physical body or where they will go when the body no longer exists. A deep-rooted fear of death can be suppressed for many years, but with spiritual transformation, curious stirrings about death begin to reveal themselves.

Delving into material to investigate what death could be, as we begin to read about death and dying and dialogue about it with others, reveals a knowing that death is a beginning and not an end. The vast literature on near-death experiences teaches us that there is something more than what the physical body alone has sensed. This realization is made concrete within us when we can see, know, and feel for ourselves that there is so much more than just a physical world. We come to know that people and all their relationships change form upon death, but they never end. People do not die, they are simply released into another form; this is the world that we come to glimpse with our new perceptions. This is the other world that has been written about for eons. This is the world that becomes our new world when we are released from the body. This is the world we get to know as *Homo nuovo* where the boundary between the physical world and the other world becomes very thin. Death then is seen as release from one state to another and is not based on punishment or judgment. It is simply a life that continues to exist and transform and change, with its ultimate purpose of infinite spiritual growth.

As new perceptions develop, they bring a new source of love and understanding for all things. When we open ourselves to novel information then new experiences can unfold. Life begins to change one step at a time. We see a bigger purpose in life's everyday events and we see, know, and feel the forces that are gently guiding us to our highest path within those events.

CHAPTER 13

LIVING AS A SPIRITUAL BEING

To Walt, with whom I have shared many lifetimes.

TRANSFORMATION BRINGS WITH it the recognition that the meaning we assign to events in the world determines how we react in relation to them. We can see a life-threatening illness as a cause for great suffering or we decide that it is the great gift that brings lessons that could not be learned any other way. As we actively participate in how events are dealt with, we begin to recognize that every interaction in the physical world is an opportunity. We can either choose to see these as opportunities for growth or we choose to remain unaltered by them. If we accept the invitation for change and a lesson is learned from each event, then life situations move in a new direction, and new opportunities are presented. If we choose to not learn the lessons then the same opportunities will present themselves, over and over again with the same result in the end. Difficult clients show up at work and though they may they have different names and appearances, the same characters continuously appear. This is how the environment provides opportunities for each of us to see ourselves in others and to create new, higher evolved forms of ourselves.

One particular man may find himself always having problems when traveling. He finds his flights are constantly delayed, traffic is backed up when he is trying to get to a destination on time, there are numerous errors made by others when booking trains and plane tickets. It seems that this occurs frustratingly often for him yet others do not have this persistent problem. A woman finds herself in one relationship after another with what appears to be the same type of man. The relationships always begin with great hope, falling in love, and a feeling that this is the special one for the rest of her life. Within months she finds herself yet again feeling empty and unfulfilled; she sees the men as distant and uncaring. No matter who it is or how they behave, the relationships always end up the same in the end.

Eventually every situation brings the realization that interactions in the physical world are opportunities to grow in the spiritual dimension. Every interaction with neighbors or coworkers, every interaction with one's children, every stranger in an elevator: they are all providing life lessons for spiritual advancement. In fact, it becomes abundantly clear that there is an intelligence participating in all things that is conspiring for each and every one's upliftment.

To evolve into a Spiritual Being means there is the conscious choice to see the opportunities that present themselves and to actively participate in them. Rather than name-calling a difficult coworker we begin to look within to see why we attracted this situation and what needs to be learned. Rather than taking revenge on someone who has caused harm, we try to look at the situation from a higher perspective. We see the hypercritical, angry boss in a new light that is calling us to change our own attitude rather than waiting for a change in her. We also come to accept the fact that if we do not live consciously and learn what needs to be learned, life simply stays the same.

Not evolving means we continue to have life events repeat themselves over and over again. The people may change, the job may change, but the painful interactions are still embedded there. Relationships with our own children continue to bring heartache. Chronic health problems bring nothing but repeated disappointment. It is only when we are tired of the same painful life situations and actively want a more peaceful and joyful life that the spiritual path is consciously taken.

Triggers that alert us to possible situations that can accelerate transformation are those we particularly want to avoid. Perhaps visiting our mother brings crazy-making drama. Spending time with our family may bring guilt and anxiety. Having to face an old friend activates the emotions of betrayal and hatred buried there many years before. These are the very situations where a deep life lesson for transforming is potentially held. These are the opportunities to acquire new attitudes and new meaning. This also triggers the possibility of helping us break our old patterns in our current lives.

When we finally make amends with the mother who was not emotionally available to us as a child and inevitably left a dark hole deep inside the self, then we are finally able to find our own source of love inside ourselves. If we have the courage to face the people we have betrayed then the veil of guilt can be lifted and self-regard can be had. Indeed it takes courage to face those people and places that conjure up all our greatest fears and pain but by not facing them, we keep them alive and ourselves stagnant.

So those on the path to *Homo nuovo* begin working with the levels of self to develop a spiritual orientation, at the physical, mental, emotional, and spiritual planes. This is undertaken with excitement and perhaps a bit of trepidation, as the path is new ground. As each little step is taken there are tremendous rewards in a life filled with deep love and joy, which blossoms in a way that has never been experienced before.

We consciously connect to others through an understanding that each situation is for higher learning and higher evolution. We recognize that we are either moving away from being a higher evolved human or toward it with every thought and action. We accept that doing the same old things and having the same old thoughts and feelings generates the same old results. One way to keep us consciously connected to our own lives is to develop a personal practice that keeps us focused on our growth, no matter what we are facing in the physical world.

It is important to note that a personal practice cannot be dictated by anyone else. There are certainly people who can help and guide us or make suggestions but, ultimately, a spiritual practice is based on personal choice. Some may choose to go to church, synagogue, or groups for meditation and prayer. Others may not. Some may choose art or music as a medium for connection, while others may find travel is their venue for transformation. No matter what form the practice takes, it is important to be undertaken as a daily routine and eventually, it is lived in each moment of life. The practice becomes who we are.

When exploring one's own spiritual practice it is important to keep focused on spiritual balance. That is, choosing a practice that is right but also one that fits into the realm of life that respects others. A practice that asks great sacrifice of the self or others is not one that uplifts anyone on their spiritual journey. We know we have chosen a correct path by how it feels but also how it uplifts everyone around us at the same time.

We also come to know that as we change and transform, the practice will change and transform as well. For this reason, it is often necessary to seek out new ways to connect and deepen our connection with our own source of love. As we connect deeply we learn that spiritual evolution does not happen in the head; it happens in the heart. By actively keeping this connection within ourselves and then outwardly sharing it with others, we keep our balance in life. It is no longer enough to just think or talk about what a spiritual connection is, or what it might be. We begin living it fully, one moment at a time.

PART II

Steps Toward Spiritual Growth

INTRODUCTION

WE CAN NOW think of the Spiritual Being as living at four different but equally important levels. The level of the physical body itself, and the environment around each and every one of us, is one level of existence. This is the level we are perhaps most aware of because we can see, smell, feel, hear, and touch the sensations in the environment. This includes our bodies, our homes, our belongings, and everyone and everything we are in physical contact with. The second is the emotional level, which is how we feel. This is the life inside each of us that is constantly telling us about the world. The third is the mental level, the ability to think and reason. While most people spend most of their waking day in this level, we must remember it is just one of four and the other levels are of equal importance. The level at which the physical, emotional, and mental levels come together is the spiritual level, where they all connect and become something greater than each alone.

The path to spiritual transformation is one from the five-sensory human, who lives mainly at the physical, emotional, and mental levels, to *Homo nuovo*, one who lives with all five senses and more. The transformation also entails living at all four dimensions by giving each of them attention with conscious awareness. We move away from over-focusing on pleasing the sensations of the physical body with stimulants and material pleasures in order to make room for the other levels. We stop giving our physical body more attention than our mind or emotions. Developing a balance between all the levels of being is the goal of transformation. With balance in mind, we do not meditate and pray to the exclusion of physical self-care and meaningful work. The secret to healthy transformation is finding time and space for all levels of one's own being. It is in this balance that transformation can occur, but also, where it can accelerate at a boundless pace.

Set forth here are some suggestions for aiding in the transformation to *Homo nuovo*, and they are exactly that. They are not laws or rules or things anyone must do. There is nothing we must do; only we ourselves know what is needed and what it desired, and we know this is by how it feels. Our true journey inward is one that provides challenges but also relief and a deep sense of inner peace. On this path, no one can tell another how they must progress, but what we can do is simply share the experiences that have occurred on the voyage.

The ideas set forth here lay the groundwork for anyone wishing to consciously choose to grow and change at the physical, emotional, mental, and spiritual levels. Countless people have already begun this process through various religions or the vast literature depicting spiritual paths. Popular spiritual writers have helped many find their way toward exploring their spiritual quest and practice. Yoga, meditation, Chi gong, and other venues have certainly guided people toward *Homo nuovo*. Though reading, meditating, sharing, and personal rituals are all important aspects for transformation, it seems these alone are not enough. Transformation seems to occur, and certainly accelerates, when one actively participates in it, on a moment-by-moment basis. It is not enough to have a weekly or even daily ritual, but rather, the practice becomes living in awareness at each and every moment of life.

Reading material about the topic of spirituality, discussing it, going to seminars, watching movies on the topic can all be instrumental in helping us learn about the various spiritual dimensions. Participating in these and then moving to the next book or event is part of the process of transformation but then, there eventually comes a time when we need to develop a practice that keeps us evolving and moving forward in every moment. Developing a unique and personal practice will keep us fully connected to something greater than ourselves and to stay connected to that essence to the best of our ability. This is truly the path to *Homo nuovo*; we begin to become that which we know.

As we hone the skills of our own practice we begin to have a strong feeling of trust when things do not go the way we think they should. A larger picture develops where we can stand back and become aware. There is a feeling that a much bigger purpose to all things is at play, even though we may not fully understand what that purpose is. Over time we can stand in our fear, anxiety, or any negative emotion and trust that circumstances will play out as they should; a great inner strength begins to mature.

As we fully trust the process and have a commitment to transformation, we give birth to a loving connection deep inside of ourselves in a way we have not felt before. This new connection keeps us in balance, no matter what worldly situations may look like. Along with this commitment comes a joy and upliftment, which, in itself, is the reward that keeps us committed to the practice. As the practice accelerates the process of change, the changes in turn continue to bring more joy, more life fulfillment, and a deeper sense of meaning than ever before. The spiral toward *Homo nuovo* moves faster and the rewards are greater with each and every moment of our journey.

It must be noted, however, that the demands of everyday life may not necessarily look different at all and the steps toward spiritual growth can be very small. Taking small steps one at a time is often how the transformation occurs. Relationships continue to happen, employment is still a physical reality, family is still family. What changes are the inner resources that help us to maneuver and navigate through the difficult demands of everyday living with spiritual development as the focal point. Everything is seen through new eyes and, eventually, more than five senses are used to see and know and feel why situations are arising in one's life as they are.

Through all the changes we also realize that we are all still in the human experience. The goal then is to grow and change in a positive way but to also know that backsliding now and then is part of the growth and to fully accept this. Choices that do not uplift or fall in line with one's committed practice can occur, but when this is realized, new choices are made. The path is not taken perfectly or in a straight line. At times we may forget we wanted to transform until something jolts us back on our way. This may be the development of an unusual skill or a life crisis. Either way, we get back to our transformation when we are ready to move forward again.

So there is acceptance in the process of being human while moving toward something new. The operative word is "moving," knowing there is no perfect way to transform and no demands on how this is done. The process of change is simply to accept it, choose the right personal path, and begin living it, moment by moment. After weeks, months, and years of making changes with each thought and action as best we can, the transformation into a Spiritual Being unfolds. We put one foot in front of the other and make a decision in each moment as best we can. Difficult challenges in life will happen. Things will happen that we cannot understand or cope with well at times. People and situations will pose challenges and these will not always be dealt with in a positive manner. This is normal. What is important is that we each remain committed to our own spiritual growth within our own unique spiritual practice, turning love and compassion toward the self.

Finally, two notions to be kept at the forefront of the mind is that everyone moves toward becoming a Spiritual Being at their own pace, and that the process must be experienced and tested by each and every person. While one person may find dreams to be guiding and precognitive, another may find a particular religious affiliation and music to be the most beneficial path. Someone else may find that working in a helping profession and reading spiritual books is the key to transformation; yet another may find yoga and meditation is the path that resonates. Most importantly, each of us must prove the process to ourselves. We try on new modalities and see what works and what does not work. One of the greatest benefits of transformation is that each individual can, and should, put all practices to the test. If attending a particular church feels uplifting and beneficial then that should be continued. If it feels oppressive and isolating then it needs to be reconsidered. Perhaps yoga is a way to feel fulfilled but if in time the practice loses its appeal then it may have to be replaced with a new-found ritual. The beauty of finding one's own spiritual balance is that numerous paths can be explored and we each find that which suits us best. The journey to *Homo nuovo* is one with many roads but they all eventually lead to the very same place.

When exploring and creating a practice it is best to keep it fresh and fun. We can do this by reading books of many genres to open the mind. New practices such as joining dance or painting classes, group meditation, gardening, or learning to play a musical instrument are all joyful paths to going within. Sharing time with friends, working at a local soup kitchen, running a charity, spending time with children; the options to designing one's own personal practice are endless. The joy, the wonder, and fun begin in a way we have never experienced before.

CHAPTER 14

PHYSICAL FLUCTUATIONS

––––––––

To Matthew, who has taught me the powerful force of love.

THE PHYSICAL BODY is perhaps the most basic level of human existence. It is with and through the body that life is felt and lived. It is with the body that the emotions can resonate and that the world can be sensed. The physical body is of utmost importance in being alive and sensing the world because it is the filter for each and every person to have their experiences through. It is through the skin, the sensory organs, the heart, and all other aspects of this form that sensing and feeling the world is experienced. Though this is the basic existence of humans, and the apparatus between the world and experiencing the world, it is also the one state that is often ignored or abused. How can the world and life be fully experienced through a damaged or neglected filter?

One of the most valuable features in the process toward *Homo nuovo* is to begin eating natural and unprocessed foods. The body literally takes food and turns it into cells, blood, organs, and all physical matter. Skin, hair, nails, the heart, the liver; everything is built from food that is ingested. Food literally becomes the tissue that life can flow through so, the more natural the food that is ingested, the more natural the body will be. If toxins are ingested in the form of processed or unnatural foods then the body will be contaminated with these toxins. The result is a body that distorts information from the world through the senses, becoming slow and sluggish, and unable to live fully and actively in the world. When a body is nourished with fresh, natural, organic foods, it becomes the perfect filter between the physical world and the inner experiences.

There is also a caution to not overeat, which has become the habit in many countries and is a growing trend around the world. Eating for entertainment, to numb uncomfortable feelings, or to feed a hunger that has nothing to do with food should be avoided. The relationship to food should be a sacred one where it is understood that food nourishes the body. If certain foods are not nourishing then eating is not about sustenance but about something that is not related to the purpose of food. A closer look at this may be warranted and when a healthy relationship to food develops in the mind, then new food choices are made. We can reflect on our own spiritual advancement by how healthy our relationship is to the very stuff that we become.

Much attention is now being given to water and global sources of water, which is imperative because this is also the very substance that the human body comes to be. Water acts as a carrier of life to the body it is hydrating. More and more people are drinking unnatural substances such as chemically made sodas, juices with foreign agents and additives, and other beverages that are unnatural to the body. These are liquids that cannot replace water. Water in its natural form, with no vitamins, minerals, toxins, or additives, is what the body needs. Pure and simple. Giving the body water throughout the day is a consideration for adding to one's practice of transformation since the better the state of the body, the better transformation can occur.

A second feature of *Homo nuovo* is the need to greatly limit or eliminate alcohol. Alcohol changes sensations and perceptions so they become distorted. By decreasing the amount of alcohol ingested, the senses become more acute, so a natural inclination is to decrease the ingestion of alcohol, which allows for a clearer experience of the world at all times. Though small amounts may still be desired or even desirable, the move away from large amounts of alcohol seems to be a natural process. The body may begin responding in a negative manner with illness or pain even to minute amounts of alcohol, which is a sign that this substance is not wanted or tolerated by the changing body.

The same can be said for illicit drugs, which, when removed from the human experience, leave a more natural relationship between the body and the world. It is often argued that drugs can enhance the spiritual experience especially beyond the five senses and though this may be true, the deleterious effects far outweigh any benefits that drugs may have. Drugs may be a fast-tracking way to experience spiritual awareness that will only occur in a temporary fashion, and dissipates once the drug loses its effect. The deleterious effects must be seriously considered and they often outweigh the fact that we cannot replace the moment-by-moment experience of a committed spiritual practice with anything but our own effort.

An exception to this may be plant medicines used throughout the world to aid in experiencing spiritual realms. These are not, however, street drugs, but are shamanic medicines that are used with the assistance and guidance of ancient wisdom. The shaman is trained in understanding what occurs with the medicine and can guide the user to a purposeful life through the experiences. This is in far contrast to street drugs that are made from some unknown origin and carry the energy of deceit, dishonesty, and greed.

Prescription and over-the-counter drugs should also be ingested with caution since they too alter the human experience away from its natural state. There is a growing dependence on these unnatural substances as they are often administered in childhood and become the normal pattern into adulthood. The body moves further and further away from its original state when foreign chemicals are ingested. Of course there are times when these are necessary for survival or comfort, but using them judiciously is wise in order to keep the body as clean a filter as possible. Balance is the objective. Keeping in mind that the body is to be treated with respect and to be honored is a great reminder of what it needs.

The physical body was also meant to move. When it is not walking, running, stretching, and bending regularly, it does not function very well. Though movement is essential, more and more people are choosing to live sedentary lives. Choosing to have movement in one's life each and every day is vital for *Homo nuovo*. How physical movement occurs is a personal preference and as varied as there are practices. Playing a sport may bring the exact body conditioning that is right for one person but yoga may be right for another. Walking through the busy streets of a crowded city may be perfect for someone else, while a job requiring physical labor may keep another in perfect balance. Whatever the choice for keeping the body moving, we know it is right because along with food choices, the body finds its own equilibrium in terms of wellness and ideal body fat. If we store and carry more fat than is natural, this too will cause it to be an imperfect filter for the senses and for transformation.

If an exercise program is chosen as part of one's practice then this should be undertaken in a natural way. If substances or exercises are used to enhance one's physical body for vanity, then this is not likely a feature for spiritual upliftment. The underlying intentions for exercise such as keeping the body sexually attractive or for feeling superior to others should be made conscious. Similarly, using exercise to numb feelings that need to be dealt with also should be put into awareness. The practice of exercise and movement then becomes about honoring the body and keeping it in its natural state for the purpose of wellness and spiritual fulfillment.

Equally important are the physical spaces we spend our time in, which affect the body greatly. The body needs to spend time outdoors where the senses can interact with fresh air and sunlight. The natural environment has much to offer the transforming body and these interactions are essential in the transformational process. There is a reason that churches and temples over the centuries have beautiful gardens and outdoor settings. The entire human body changes when in the midst of nature; flowers, trees, birds, the wind, and sunlight are all beneficial to us and should be considered when choosing one's daily practice. Even in crowded cities one can choose to walk in a park or to simply be in the busy streets soaking up the sun and the elements.

While spending time outdoors, we can become cognizant to have direct contact with the earth itself, which is called *grounding*. Grounding is achieved by having bare feet directly touching the earth by walking on grass, sand, or soil. The reason this is so beneficial is that the earth itself has an electromagnetic resonance, which happens to be that of the natural rhythm of the human body. By having direct contact with the earth through the feet, the human body can become recalibrated by the earth. We get thrown off our natural rhythm by interacting in the world with negative emotions, fatigue, and stress. This can also occur by being exposed to pollution or multiple forms of electromagnetic radiation such as mobile phone use, mobile phone towers, and wireless Internet. Grounding is a phenomenal method for naturally balancing the body that has become lost in many cultures around the planet. If environments are not conducive to walking barefoot because there are no exposed areas of grass or soil, or it is simply too cold for direct contact with the earth, then a similar grounding effect occurs by soaking one's feet in water with natural sea salts. This simple yet valuable exercise can bring great rewards to all human bodies of all cultures, ages, and levels of wellness.

Perhaps one of the greatest challenges to the physical body is that of illness or physical pain. Once this sets into the cells, then everything changes and can be challenging in a multitude of ways. It is wise to seek out all options for healing the body at this level since there are so many opportunities available globally. Certainly medicines, surgery if needed, alternative healing methods, energy medicine, and other modalities should all be explored. When the body has become ill or in pain, then restoring it back to a healthy state becomes of utmost importance.

When physical conditions are beyond repair or one's birth state, then the illness is not signaling a need for correction, but a need for acceptance and a new paradigm of what wellness is. In many cases, whether the condition is temporary or permanent, one option for healing is to explore the condition as an opportunity for personal and spiritual growth.

From a very young age we are often taught that illness is a bad thing and this moves through global consciousness with the domino effect. Media sensationalizes the deleterious effects of illness, which fuels the fire that it is all bad. When we adopt this view of illness, we set the stage for the ego to play out its drama and be fed by giving in to it and showing everyone around us how bad life is. Of course this also has a domino effect and then everyone involved adopts the view of the illness that best suits their ego drama as well.

People with the same illness may unconsciously adopt the "this is a horrible thing" mentality and spread it around the globe. Some people will try to deny or minimize that the illness even exists because they are afraid someone with the illness will get more attention than they are getting. Others may behave negatively because they feel that, by their own actions, they have contributed to the existence of the illness. Others may feed into the illness so they can become the victim and fuel their own needs in this way. The damaging effects of the negative mindset of illness can be far reaching and continuous, gaining momentum with each repetition. Others will suffer more than the person with the illness because this plays into their own emotional pain that has not been dealt with. Our suffering and our attempts to make others suffer in order to share our pain are two ways to deal with illness. Perhaps we can consider another way.

As we begin to transform, illness and pain can also be seen as a "messenger" for spiritual growth. What does this illness mean? What can I learn from this? Why is this occurring in my life? What major changes do I need to make in order to heal fully? Illness then becomes a call to go inward, where new answers for healing may lie.

A woman who develops breast cancer may find that she has lived a very unconscious life and has made choices that caused her to block love to her own children. Another woman with colon cancer may find that her illness shows her that she must let go of controlling life and let life flow more as it may. A man with heart disease may discover in his journey inward that he has not loved anyone fully because he was too busy judging and feeling judged. Each and every person will find an answer to their own physical ailment and, from there, the transformational process can unfold. Illness is often one of the major catalysts of spiritual transformation, if we can allow it to do its work.

While exploring one's personal spiritual path by going inward, it seems important to also look at living spaces. When we create living environments that are clean, orderly, and pleasing to all the senses this seems to enhance the process. A place that will allow the new emerging self to grow and gently reveal itself is a necessity. Even barren and simple environments can fulfill this purpose, often more so than those with much adornments. For some people, it may take just a few quiet minutes away from a chaotic home to begin feeling the transformation that is gently occurring. For others, it is lighting a candle and sitting in a quiet space. Whatever the form the environment takes, be it a park bench, a meditation room, a yoga studio, or time spent in a bookstore, it is a safe haven that provides a peaceful refuge.

While finding this safe space, it is essential to decrease the input of sensory information from chaos and excessive noise and allow the self-appropriate space to grow and change. If we can make this space for our own awareness to develop on a regular basis, then other senses can emerge from this peaceful place. This is often how we develop the awareness beyond our five senses in a far richer and deeper way. This metasensory perception is a major feature of *Homo nuovo*, which emerges in each distinctive environment that we create.

Some will begin to see a realm of existence not seen with the eyes such as auras of light around living things or sensing images of the deceased. Others will begin to sense the emotions and intentions of others. Negative states in others such as lying or being deceitful are intentions that seem palatable to those with metasensory perception. Yet others will smell impending death or feel it at a deep level of knowing from someone around them. These senses are becoming more and more common as people emerge into *Homo nuovo* en masse. The boundary between the self and others gets thinner and thinner as the new senses begin to blossom.

These new senses are often called *subtle senses* because they are very quiet, very low, and below the radar of our usual sensing. One must be very still and often in near silence to see, know, or feel this emerging state. These states are also as varied as there are humans transforming. It seems that each individual will acquire senses that are unique and appropriate to their own lives. One person may develop the ability to sense impending death because her life's purpose is to help people cross over when it is their time. Another may develop the sense of feeling other people's feelings because his purpose is to help with the emotional healing of others. Someone else develops the skill of precognitive dreaming in order to make a contribution to society with that information. As the skills develop in their unique way they are often entwined with one's life work and greater purpose. These skills can be used and shared for the benefit of others, which, in turn, accelerate the transformation of the skill. We can encourage this transformation by becoming fully aware of the physical spaces in which we choose to live that either aid or hinder the development of this new awareness. An environment that nurtures the development of new skills will be one where information is clear and flows cleanly to the metasensory level. Environments that are not conducive to progress will result in the physical world being experienced just as it always has been.

As the environment becomes a space for spiritual change, then the ability to enjoy beautiful things in the environment also seems to increase. Beautiful artwork, clothing that enhances the body, a flowering plant, a glimpse of crystal in the sunlight. Everything pleasing to the senses becomes more so, and a deep sense of awe is eventually cultivated.

Interestingly, while beautiful things become more beautiful by paying attention to them, the need to minimize the attachment to materialism slowly occurs. It's perfectly fine to have material things and to enjoy them but material things are often given more value than are people and human connection. We now see people in restaurants who are completely engrossed on their mobile phones while unaware of the companion across from them. Children are living in fantasy realms of games and make-believe that get them addicted to contrived worlds. They ignore their siblings and friends to stay connected to a world that does not exist for their ultimate upliftment. When we take time away from technology daily to not answer the phone, watch TV, play video games, or engross ourselves in the Internet, we unplug to spend time with ourselves. When we consciously move our attention away from material objects of any kind and venture inward to the self, we find a world that provides many more rewards than any object can. The key is to give the inner life a chance to reveal itself and for us to begin befriending it.

The true self, deep inside our core, is often hidden because it has been ignored for so long. It has been bombarded with the loud sounds of music or television. It has been numbed out with chemically-laced food, alcohol, and drugs. The small quiet voice within will slowly emerge if it is given a chance. In order to transform ourselves we have to cooperate with our process and life on this planet. As we provide environments conducive to our personal transformation, we can listen for the whispering messages that are so very subtle, and which we can only hear in nurturing venues.

We then expand our view of what encompasses our entire environment and we see that it not only includes our home, but everything around us. The park across the road becomes a place that is important to us. The busy street that we share with others is important to us. The school grounds where the children play take on a new meaning. Everything in our physical world becomes sacred territory for it is the place for each of us to grow and transform. We begin to understand the impact each of us has on our environment and we take responsibility for our part. Our role then is to not change others but to simply allow ourselves to change, which in turn, helps the whole world to change.

Finally is the notion that all physical bodies eventually end in the experience of death. Though perhaps this is the most difficult concept for most people to accept, it becomes much easier with spiritual transformation. As we transform ourselves at every level of being, we come to understand that there is no death, but only a release from one state of being to another. The true essence of being human is discovered in *Homo nuovo*, and with it the realization that death means that life continues on from one realm to another. Life never ends. The part of us responsible for thinking and animating the body is released, intact, continuing to think and interact in another space. We are on a continuous journey of never-ending change and advancement to greater forms of ourselves. What we make of ourselves in this life is what we will be upon death. If we are full of love and compassion at the time we release from the body, then that is where we begin the next phase of our existence. If we are angry and full of hatred then this will be the starting point of life in the next realm. Everything we are at the point of death is what we bring forward.

By keeping this in mind, we come to see that every moment of life in the human form matters. It matters in terms of how our lives continue beyond this one and where we begin the next journey. This life then is preparation for the next, in whatever form we choose it to take.

So as life continues from one realm to the next, each and every one of us is actually a cell in the entire body of creation. As we advance ourselves through our choices, the entire system advances also. As each one of us becomes a little more evolved, the entire universe becomes a little more evolved; there is only one life form in the entire universe and we are a part of it.

Once we are on the path of developing metasensory skills and we know that life is constantly transforming into many states upon death, then the ability to see, know, and feel these other states becomes developed also. An active relationship can develop with a deceased parent with a mere thought. Guidance and direction can be provided from a deceased child through a felt sense. As the boundary between the physical world and the other worlds becomes thinner, the interaction between worlds becomes actively possible. A human life doesn't exist solely to work, strive, and survive; rather, it has a much richer and deeper purpose. Each of us comes to realize our place in the universe as a unique essence that is contributing to the whole of creation with every thought, word, and action we take.

EMOTIONAL EXPRESSIONS

––––––––

*To Anthony, whose soul is entwined with
mine in many mysterious ways.*

ONE OF THE means by which we transform our entire way of being is by minding our inner life: the emotions that rise and fall in a constant flow. As we begin to keep track of our own feelings we can observe how our emotions move inside of us. The reason for this is so negative feelings do not get rooted, or take a firm hold, which can then get control of our lives. Secondly, spiritual insights come with understanding our own emotional life. As we look within, we see the layers of conditioning that have clouded our true essence. Our feelings are the gateway to freedom for they will lead us to the blocks of our true self. It is important then to come to know the ones we can plainly see in ourselves and the ones hidden deep in the unconscious mind.

By watching our own emotional reactions we come to see that most of us are reacting to life situations in the same manner over and over again. We may catch ourselves often feeling afraid. We may see that we often get angry. We feel a churning of worry in the pit of our stomachs. When we begin to see these patterns as part of ourselves, we can examine them and begin having a different reaction. We do not have to choose the same emotion over and over again, keeping us the same. People will often say, "But this is who I am." In reality, we are what we choose to be, whether we realize it or not. Once the choice is made to react differently to life situations, then we begin to break out of our old mold and transform. This can occur with one emotional choice at a time.

As we watch our reactions and begin catching ourselves before we react, we can see and feel a different emotional life inside ourselves. Another way to shift our emotions is to adjust the body into the position of the inner feeling we wish to have. If we wish to become happy we can smile, hold our head a bit higher, and press the shoulders back. Once the body is in this position for feeling happy the emotions that accompany this stance will naturally be expressed. When we learn to move the body into new positions, we feel ourselves changing, and people begin to treat us differently. It seems that when we change, everything and everyone begins to change with us.

What, however, do we do with those emotions that are buried deep, so deep, that we are unaware of them? One way we can detect these hidden feelings is to watch how we react to other people. When we react emotionally to others we are projecting onto them what we ourselves are feeling, yet we are completely unaware that this exists inside of us. People become the perfect mirror for us to see what we are on the inside. When a woman angrily talks about her sister-in-law's lying and cheating it is because she needs to look at this behavior in herself. If a man is repeatedly jealous of other men around his wife he needs to look at his own thoughts of lust and infidelity with other women. So the emotions and labels we put onto others that stir our own deep emotions are signals to look within. If we see deceit in another we must look at the deceit hidden within; we are seeing others as we are and not how they are. On the other hand, if we simply see the neighbor playing out her ego drama with games of dishonesty and we do not have issues of our own dishonesty hidden from us, then we will not be emotionally moved in any way. We see it for what it is as a simple observation. It is only upon strong emotional reactions that we reflect on what is hidden and acting as a trigger. What is it that we have to look at inside ourselves that is pushing its way through to conscious awareness?

Defensiveness is another sure sign that a hidden emotion is trying to rear its head. When someone says something and we react defensively, this is a valuable lesson on recognizing our emotional layers. If someone says we are stubborn and we emotionally react to that, then the stubbornness has revealed itself! If someone accuses us of being untruthful and we react, then our untruthfulness has been uncovered. These emotions can no longer hide in the recesses of our being. Our own defensiveness then is a great friend. It gives us the gift of becoming conscious to those parts of ourselves that want to stay hidden and want to control our lives beyond our control. The more we befriend defensiveness in ourselves and learn about our inner world, the faster we can spiritually transform.

So we begin to know and understand our own emotional lives, which is the force that is moving us through our days. As part of this process, we may choose to look deeply into our emotional reactions and pain with the help of trained professionals. Seeking out professional help with therapists, groups, guided meditation leaders, or the multitude of tools known to explore the emotional landscape, can be a valuable asset when choosing our spiritual practice. By exploring the emotions and slowly transmuting or transforming them, we slowly transform ourselves. It seems that the deeper the emotions lie and the more pain they have caused, the greater the opportunity for moving toward joy, bliss, and gratitude.

Fear is one of the principal emotions that can debilitate the natural flow of life. When fear sets in, it acts as a massive block to thinking in adaptive ways and sensing the world in a positive light. Fear acts as a filter so stimuli from the outside world enter into the mind and body in a distorted way. Fear can propagate itself so simple stimuli such as a sunny day or a walk with a friend becomes a barrage of pain created by the body. Of course this emotion grows on itself so the fear of a frightened reaction becomes the worst trigger of all. No matter how big or how small the situation that elicits fear may be, it has some control over one's life and continues to do so when left to its own devices. It is a great day when the choice is made by one person to face their fear and slowly allow it to dissipate. The effects of this are far-reaching since everyone who is in contact with that fear may experience a negative consequence because of it. When any level of fear begins to dissipate its negative effects also dissipate, which means the domino effect is lessened to a large degree.

The dark blanket of sadness that is often entwined with hostility can become the debilitating emotion of depression. This too feeds back onto itself as the negative views of the self, others, and the world take hold and fuel the cycle of depression. The deeply painful waves of this emotion can kill the will and the life force of anyone it gets ahold of. If we are able to look at the depressive state and what has caused it to reside inside the body, then the blanket of darkness can begin lifting. Depression is often rooted in an early life experience that cannot be easily dislodged so experiences of the past continue to live in the present by reverberating within the human body. So it is by seeking professional help, combined with self-guided emotional work, that depression begins to reveal its gifts. The gift of incredible transformation can be illuminated from the dark side of this painful human experience. We need the courage to go within and allow the emotion to do its work.

The best friend of depression, that which accompanies depression as often as is possible, is anxiety. This feeling is felt physically in the body with tension, sweating, dizziness, and a myriad of other symptoms. Often anxiety comes from the unconscious mind knowing that something is wrong and the feeling is not allowed to have its say. Knowing at a deep level that a partner is being unfaithful yet the truth is being hidden and buried in one's own self can cause symptoms of anxiety to arise. Knowing that an illness has set into the body but rather than facing it, burying the fear of the illness down into the layers of the mind, will plant the seeds of anxiety. Anxiety is like a valve that is allowing the true, tumultuous feelings to reveal themselves by coming to the surface. These feelings are boiling deep in the mind and the body and cannot be held down for long. The more we try to hold those feelings down, the more the valve of anxiety will try to burst open. Shaking, worrying, fear, and hyperarousal are all signs that some emotion is trying to have its say. The symptoms will continue to manifest until the root cause is unveiled. With professional guidance, working on the inner life, and finding the past trigger that is being carried into future events, anxiety can be one of the greatest springboards of transformation. Not only does anxiety help with major insights but, should it return, it is a constant reminder that the inner journey must be made again and again.

Hostility, rage, and anger are the emotional voices screaming out that there is something in life that we do not want. A father who raged and physically hurt his family, a mother who drank alcohol to the point of not knowing she had a family around her, a neighbor who couldn't control his lust for a child and transgressed hurtfully. The anger that arises in reaction to these is a siren for inner work to be done. Often the seed of anger was planted on the inside at a very young age and we are completely unaware of its existence. We don't know where it was planted and by whom. Anger can grow when it is left unattended so it comes up again and again as a calling to be given attention. It needs to be recognized for what it is: a major transformational mechanism. Anger is often the inner signal that is screaming "no." It is a way of saying I do not want this in my life. It is sometimes saying "Stop hurting me." When we listen to our own anger, it is a sign to go within and to find the life situations that need to be changed or altered. Anger has been a human protection mechanism from the beginning of time and, when left unattended, it continues to grow. Anger is an emotion that blatantly calls for attention and adjustment in the inner and outer worlds.

Many choices in human behavior bring with them a sense of shame or guilt, which are strong waves of negative emotion turned inward. This emotion usually originates from the imposition of ideas from other people such as parents, spouses, religious groups, or other society norms. Just as depression, anxiety, and anger act as springboards for spiritual transformation, this is also the case with guilt and shame. These emotions bring us back to ourselves and it is only with self-reflection that we can see what we are doing and why we are doing it. These emotions may bring to our awareness that we have transgressed a moral code. They may also bring aware-ness that control issues need to be addressed. Whatever the case, once we face these realizations, changes can begin to happen with a conscious mind fully open, resulting in shame and guilt beginning to dissolve away.

One of the most profound emotions in the human experience is that of grief from loss. When the heart is in pain from the loss of a loved one, grief is the most natural response. It is very important to grieve our losses and to allow ourselves to feel the pain from loss. If we let grief do its work throughout the body, even though it is painful, it will carve us into new beings. The greatest tendency is to numb out the emotions accompanying grief because it hurts so deeply, but also it reminds us of a life change in the loss. If we can have the courage to feel the pain of grief and combine it with the understanding that life never ends, then this is another step in reform. Facing grief courageously is a life experience that takes us to face death and the possibility of becoming a Spiritual Being as quickly as we will allow it.

As we begin to journey inward whenever we are aware of our own emotions, then often confusion about what we are feeling can occur. Emotions, with their intense energetic force, can begin to swirl into one another. We don't know if we are angry or sad. We don't know if we are feeling shame, depression, or both. Often we are feeling many emotions all at the same time and it is only by befriending and getting to know them that insights can occur. The emotional landscape can be a tumultuous one for sure, but this also holds the key to understanding ourselves and our own path to becoming something new.

When we do not work with our emotional life but let it run its own course, then we block ourselves from experiencing the world by putting up a filter. We can carry a filter of anger or frustration. We may put up a filter of sadness or anxiety, which distorts the world we are interacting with. Ultimately, these blocks act as resistance to the process of developing the multisensory perception — the perception that allows us to see, know, and feel the world in a completely different way. Avoidance of emotional work keeps us seeing the world from a purely physical perspective alone. So once we decide to actively participate in our own transformation, there are several things we can choose to do emotionally, as part of a practice.

The first step in emotional change is to recognize that the emotions are alive and well inside of the self. This is done by conscious awareness and noticing what is happening on the inside. If anger comes up we notice it. If a flash of anxiety comes up we give it our attention. Eventually this becomes a natural process and the emotions do not live a life separate from the being they exist in.

Once a negative emotion is noticed, we try to sit with it and then slowly transmute it as best we can. Often just by noticing it, the emotion will dissipate. Awareness is a great neutralizer of negative emotions. By suppressing our negative emotions, we not only keep them alive, we also give them more energy to stay alive in our body. So by noticing them and then slowly and consciously altering them, we begin to remove this energy from our system. When anger comes up we can have an internal dialogue to say that this is not wanted here. By doing this over and over again whenever we are aware of the emotion, it will slowly begin to change. We can look deeply at our depression and begin adding an internal stream of light to it so it cannot live inside us as a dark cloud. The process is to acknowledge, notice, and then transmute the negative emotion to allow for more positive energy to come in. The process requires consistency and vigilance so the old patterns of emotions do not set in again.

It is often helpful to consciously choose to be peaceful and to not let the drama of life affect us, or hook us, as best we can. We may find that we enjoy gossiping because it stirs up negative feelings inside of us. We may watch TV shows where people are being violently harmed and we notice that this too triggers a pain inside of us that, at some level, we like to return to. When we consciously unhook from this, we are choosing a positive and more stable inner life. We move away from the addiction to inner pain by feeding our inner world with things that are uplifting or, at the very least, neutral. The reason we make this choice is that we know it is in our best spiritual interest and that we must participate in our own transformation.

One of the next steps in spiritual transformation is to get relationships in order. All relationships, from parental to romantic to casual acquaintances, can be great sources of emotional joy, pain, and most importantly, learning. We can begin to work on our relationships by minimizing negative interactions. By living with our own awareness we begin to see that others may be controlled by their own emotions because they have no awareness at all. We begin to see those who are living as automatons, completely under the control of anger, depression, or anxiety, and those who are not. As we work on ourselves, our relationships come to light and we can let go of or at least sidestep people who are simply reacting. In turn, we decrease our own reactivity by becoming the observers of others, rather than reacting to them. We come to realize that we only have control of our own emotional reactions and so emotional and spiritual transformation brings both emotional and spiritual maturity. We change our lives dramatically by changing ourselves, not by focusing on trying to change others around us.

As we begin to pay attention to our inner world and our own reactions we must also become aware that we have blind spots. These are areas of ourselves that we are completely unable to see. The man who consumes alcohol to the point of ruining his health, whose family has a blind spot to its effects, while everyone else around him can see this. The woman who gossips at work and causes negative interactions has a blind spot to her own behavior. Since we are blind to some aspect of ourselves it is very difficult to know that this is occurring, unless we become aware of our reactivity. Whenever we have an emotional reaction, there is a deep emotional issue that is demanding attention to healing; often one that we cannot or will not see. When someone is challenged for drinking too much alcohol and he reacts negatively to that, this is the blind spot being revealed. When a man is asked if he is in an abusive relationship and he reacts defensively, this is the blind spot being revealed. Reactivity then becomes a window into deeper aspects of the self and, if recognized, becomes an invaluable mechanism for spiritual growth at the emotional level.

Another exercise that can be instrumental for emotional growth is the practice of meditation. The act of sitting quietly and calming the mind of mental chatter twice a day helps to keep emotions in a calm and peaceful state. Meditation is like medicine for the mind where thoughts and emotions are tempered. Old habits are broken so anger cannot rise so quickly. Anxiety can be recognized and soothed. Confusion and bewilderment slowly settle down and clarity begins to form. When we consciously attempt to keep emotions in check we are no longer victims to them. The emotions that have been left to run wild for so many years are slowly tamed.

In the process of taming our inner world we also begin avoiding events and stimuli, such as certain TV programs or news reports, that cause negative emotional arousal. In doing this, we adopt the practice that our sense of inner peace is one of the most important things. We are making a commitment to our inner world and how we perceive the outer world. We slowly remove the lenses of anger and pain so we see the world in a different way. This is often made with a conscious commitment on our part as inner peace does not normally develop on its own.

As we practice protecting our inner world from negative stimuli we also begin to avoid negative people, places, and things that make us feel drained, empty, or bad. Negative people carry with them their own world filled with pain, which can act as a vortex to pull the goodness out of others. This negativity can exist because of deceit, dishonesty, or game-playing. People who are living miserable lives but pretend that everything is wonderful carry a negative whirlpool of underlying emotions. As we transform spiritually, we begin to feel these negative undercurrents and we recognize them for what they are: acts of deep emotional pain. We often find ourselves becoming negative in their company because their vortex has pulled us in. Their inauthentic ways are physically painful for those who are evolving spiritually. It is best to minimize our exposure to these people as much as we can. We wish them well and we move forward.

Another transformative spiritual practice is to become aware of how we treat children. Children should not be harmed, lied to, or deceived in any way. Adults often create stories for children in an attempt to mold their beliefs. Children may be told that certain people are bad in order to manipulate them. Others will be shown age-inappropriate behavior that will shock their growing consciousness. Children are often forced to grow up too fast by adults who no longer want to parent them. Whatever the behaviors, when we act with integrity and awareness with children, we in fact grow in our own integrity and awareness. This practice keeps us on track for our own spiritual growth so with the utmost respect for children we consciously create positive relationships for them and for us. We are teaching them how to treat others and how they should be treated by others.

So the emotional life becomes a great priority for those moving toward *Homo nuovo*. In fact it is the emotional life that becomes the real world for us, rather than the other world. In order to protect and work with our inner world, we do what we can every day to cultivate a healthy inner life. Whether it be lighting a candle, walking outdoors, petting the cat, looking at beautiful art, or listening to music that uplifts, we develop a practice that allows space for our emotions to reveal themselves. We surround ourselves as best we can with those things that allow the emotions to have their say so we can work with them. The practice can include formal meditation or yoga classes but can also include very simple things such as watching the sunrise or sunset. Each and every person will determine by how it feels what to include in their emotional practice. Any behavior that it is uplifting and joyful, but never harming to another in any way, may be consideration for nurturing one's emotional existence.

CHAPTER 16

MENTAL MODIFICATIONS

———

To Heather H., editor, mentor, spiritual
teacher, and cherished friend.

THE MIND IS a place where so much is happening. We relive stories of the past: good and bad. We rehearse old hurts over and over again. We create stories of great romantic affairs that will never be, but live them as if they were true. We berate ourselves and we praise ourselves. For most people, the mind is in constant chatter and never stops so for this reason, it is here that great modifications and spiritual advancement can occur. It is a simple matter of adding workings of the mind into our daily spiritual practice.

When the mind is left to its own devices and is undisciplined, it will wreak havoc. It will take control of the individual and run the life as if there is no choice. The mind chatter can torment people with its crazy-making drama played over and over again. In response to this, people will say that the drama is true. A woman may say that she repeatedly thinks about her husband's behavior because he actually is an alcoholic and is hurting her and the family. Similarly, a woman fantasizes over and over again about the perfect partner and lover rather than seeing the one she is with. A man says that thoughts about his ex-wife churn inside of him because he can't stop thinking about the terrible things she did. The mind clings to these thoughts of transgressions and plays them over and over again causing emotional pain or fantasy living.

These ruminations can lead one's life down many paths of destruction. Illness begins first as a thought and then with the right conditions, it begins to manifest. Addictions are one rampant form of illness linked to delusions of control and grandeur but also of self-hatred and self-loathing. The mind creates the perfect conditions for this illness to take hold.

Addiction is a draw to a substance or behavior that will change one's thoughts or feelings. When we don't like who we are or what we feel then we use something outside of ourselves to change us. People may become braver with the use of a substance and will do things they could not do without it. Others become the life of social gatherings where they would be quiet and humorless without it. Deep down there is a need to change the self and the thoughts that have become distorted. A deep and pervasive feeling that we do not fit in or we are so different that we have to isolate sets in. With this, there is a magnetic draw pulling us toward a substance that provides some form of relief. Often the draw is completely unconscious. The substance then distorts the mind into delusional thoughts that can perpetuate the addiction. The distorted and delusional thoughts, in turn, create a distorted version of the person that once existed. Beliefs that the substance is not harmful or even beneficial are often created. Minimizing the amount of usage is also a thought created to keep the mind from restoring itself back to its natural state. A man may begin creating self-made rules for the substance use such as drinking or drugging only on certain days. A woman may believe that having a buzz from alcohol makes her a better mother and since all her friends do it, it's perfectly acceptable. This form of mind alteration is a widespread problem globally as people are trying to escape the false reality that has been created in their minds.

Accompanying all negative emotions, no matter how they came to exist, are underlying thoughts feeding these feelings. Under depression and sadness are negative thoughts of the self, others, and the world. The lens of perception, both inward and outward, distorts the information coming in from the environment so it has a harmful slant. It is these underlying thoughts feeding the emotions that then feed our behavior. This cycle can be broken as we transform spiritually, leaving a space for calmness and inner peace to begin to reside.

The practice of change begins by watching thoughts as they arise and starting to understand and befriend the landscape of the mind. People live many years of their lives not knowing their own thoughts. For this reason, thoughts run rampant and can run the show. After many years of letting thoughts tread their paths through the mind, it becomes nearly impossible to stop them. It is then that medications are often needed to stop the thoughts that fuel the deleterious emotions. Rather than letting it go that far, we begin to gain some control over the thoughts ourselves. We watch them. We listen to them. We become aware of this level of life that has been ignored for so long.

Once we begin watching our own thoughts then we can actively try to stop the ones that cause harm. We do not need to replay horrible traumas, real or created, over and over again. We can be more compassionate to ourselves by not repeating that cycle of storytelling. If we can stop or even distract the mind away from painful thoughts and memories, we can begin creating a new way of being, one that that is not constantly generating pain for us from the inside.

As we watch our stream of thoughts, we can also choose to replace negative mind chatter with positive thoughts. If these are too difficult to conjure up, then we can at least put the mind in neutral. We can consciously choose to say no to old hurts and new fantasies of pain. Since thoughts feed our feelings, we begin working at two levels. By not having negative thoughts, we are not creating food for negative feelings. As both the mind and the emotions begin to change, then the body also changes. Positive thoughts and feelings bring calmness and peace to the actual cells of the body. We can literally see ourselves looking and feeling more vigorous and youthful. We begin coping with life challenges in more adaptive ways.

Another level of destructive mind chatter can come in the form of self-talk. As we observe our inner dialogue we can begin to weed out thoughts that are damaging to anyone or anything. We begin to hear our own discussions about how terrible we are or the world is. We hear ourselves complaining or criticizing other people. All of this dialogue will reverberate in the mind and the body with adverse effects. Negativity in any form can only bring negative outcomes.

If we choose to add meditation into our daily practice to calm the emotions, this will also greatly calm the mind. We can let go of our old thinking, even for a short while at first, and let a new way of being unfold. Visual imagery is a form of meditative practice that allows us to rehearse situations in life as we want them to unfold. If we have a difficult coworker that we ruminate about, we can imagine that person moving away from us and not having any interactions at all during visual imagery. This form of mental work will help us in waking day to deal with situations, and thoughts about situations, differently.

While consciously choosing new thought forms throughout the day, we can also choose to occupy the mind with new ideas by reading some form of spiritual material daily. The choice of that material comes from a feeling that resonates differently for each person. Some will choose it in the form of popular novels with spiritual messages; others will choose religious doctrine; still others will find blogs and quotes uplifting. If the material leaves us feeling calm and peaceful, then it is speaking to us in a positive way, encouragingly teaching us how to evolve.

As we change our thinking with conscious awareness, we can also begin the practice of mindfulness and live in the moment as best we can. We begin to not think ahead of ourselves and, therefore, live in a past that has already happened or go into a future that has not happened yet. We live with our thoughts in the here and now. We then experience each and every moment of life rather than distracting away from the present.

As we transform our daily thoughts then we may also begin to see our sleeping mind change by the way we dream. Since dreams are the thoughts from the day continuing on during sleep, they hold rich information about our lives. They hold our deepest secrets and our hidden fears.

Keeping a dream journal is one way of getting to know our dream imagery. By writing dreams down, we bring into awareness those aspects of the self that are being exposed while the defense mechanisms are down. We can learn so much about the parts of ourselves that keep us blocked or that we keep hidden. The dreaming mind becomes an active compatriot when befriended. If we choose to delve deeper into the mind during sleep, we can also become aware of lucid dreaming and precognitive dreaming. Here the mind is helping us explore deeper aspects of the self and providing assistance in the days that lie ahead.

Conscious awareness and dreams will alert us to our own creation of drama where we complain, criticize, and point out the faults of others. These are all mechanisms that we use to focus on ego inflation by creating a false self. By catching ourselves in these behaviors we can refocus our attention back onto ourselves and what we need to do to evolve in a healthy way. By distracting our minds with gossip and the like, we are resisting the act of looking inward to what we are thinking and feeling. By noticing our own language, which is a reflection of what we are thinking, we can guide ourselves back to a transformational path rather than the old path we have worn so well.

When familiar thoughts of negativity begin to set in, and we will often know this by the anger, irritation, depression, or other negative emotions they cause, we can invite the mind to surrender. We simply let go of all the old thoughts and do not let ourselves get trapped in our own minds. We surrender to the process and slowly let our old thoughts dissipate which, in turn, decreases suffering. By not resisting our own thinking anymore we allow a new way to be cultivated.

One new way is to try to catch our thoughts about comparison to others. By comparing to other people, we measure ourselves in terms of being better or worse than someone at work. In sports we compare ourselves in terms of running faster or playing harder than a teammate. Do we make more or less money than our friends? All of these thoughts, which are often seeded in childhood, are about expanding the ego and keeping ourselves separate from others. As spiritual transformation accelerates, the need to compare and measure against others begins to diminish. When we accept that every human is on his or her own personal path then comparison becomes meaningless.

As we think and feel our way through the world, we can also hold in our awareness the repercussions of the domino effect. We hold in our minds the notion that everything we think and feel will result in a behavior that is wide-reaching. Our gossip can harm many, many others for the short-term gain of negative emotional fulfillment. All negative thoughts lead to negative feelings, which will then lead to negative behavior at some level. This chain reaction will spread like a plague to other people and from those people, to other people. We now become aware and responsible for what we are sending out to the world and we begin to live each interaction knowing there is a connection to all others.

If we think about a past hurt long enough we will begin to feel bad. This negative thought form has created a negative emotion, which can then cause us to react aggressively toward others. We may find ourselves swearing or acting aggressively to other drivers in traffic because we are carrying a negative thought form. That negativity now transfers to the other driver who reacts to it, and this initiates a negative feeling in him. Now both people carrying negative emotions go home to their families and play out their negative behavior by being miserable. One person may yell at his teenage son for something unrelated to his own negative feeling and the other stonewalls his wife by being cold and uncaring. The wife then complains to her friends about this act of injustice toward her and the teenager turns to drugs to numb out the hurt. On and on the effects of negative thoughts spread and we are all responsible for our part in that chain reaction. As we consciously feel a connection to the effects of our thoughts, feelings, and behaviors, we take responsibility for our part, which helps us to transform even faster.

One of the major changes to occur for those moving toward *Homo nuovo* is the need to judge others slowly decreases. We come to accept that we cannot know someone else's path or the life they have lived. We do not know how or why they are behaving as they are, nor do we know how this fits into their unique life and purpose. We do not know why things happen as they do for others and we are just to mind our own path, our own thoughts and feelings, and our own life. We mind our own business, so to speak. If we feel a pull to help others on their path we do so without control or without an agenda to make others think as we do.

We eventually allow ourselves to feel mentally connected to all people and all things. We consciously feel a responsibility for our part in the universe. The process to *Homo nuovo* lets us see that we are each a cell in the body of the universe and we can decide to be a healthy contributor or like an illness, spreading destruction to others and the world. Every thought then becomes of vital importance.

So what do we do then for people who are not consciously aware and behaving negatively toward us? We change our minds. For extremely difficult people and circumstances we can practice being neutral; by remaining mentally and emotionally neutral we avoid any negative effects on ourselves and thus we do not harm our own transformation. Whenever possible, we walk away and keep our spiritual balance intact as best we can.

In the process of moving toward *Homo nuovo*, we begin to see that no matter where we are or what we're doing we are never separate from others. Our connection is deeply rooted and intricately woven to all others in the world. Given this, we also begin to feel a sense of responsibility and belonging to the planet and its place in all of creation. Not just to our family, a group of friends, a town, a country, but to the entire universe.

Personal existence then becomes very purposeful and meaningful. We look at everything we do differently when on the road to spiritual transformation. Parenting becomes a sacred path as we become aware of all actions toward children. The focus of our children's well-being is not simply for our own gain or theirs, but for all the lives that our children will touch. Happy, healthy children will go out into the world and interact in a very different manner than children who are neglected or abused. We can no longer ignore the fact that our gossip will hurt the developing minds around us and beyond. We can no longer pretend that numbing out with drugs, alcohol, or any other substance or behavior does not affect children. Buying them more and more material things cannot replace the love and attention that they need to thrive. We look at ourselves as a reflection of what we are giving our children and the world at large.

The work we choose to do is also reflected on with awareness. We begin to ask how we are contributing to the well-being of others and not just ourselves. Is our work about financial gain at the expense of others? Does it only have a meaning for us other than money? Are we conducting our work while excluding the needs of others such as our family members? This too becomes a medium for growth and change as we begin to see that our ideas about our work carry forward into the world in infinite ways.

Romantic relationships can also become grounds for conscious choice and not merely need fulfilment and physical satisfaction. Our thinking begins to shift away from having one's own needs met by another, to relationships as growth experiences. We begin to ask what we are projecting onto the other person, which is really a reflection of ourselves. What areas of our personality does the other person complement and bring out that we need to become aware of? Romantic relationships can be areas of life that accelerate spiritual transformation and, interestingly, the partner does not have to be consciously involved at this level at all. When we decide to learn from our relationships then the learning is turned inward and we do not expect the other to change for us. The process of *Homo nuovo* brings the focus to us and to us alone, for it is our journey and we respect that others are on their own unique paths. Even in extreme cases where there is abuse, one has to learn to not be the abuser and the other has to learn how not to be a victim. Relationships are the perfect ground for reciprocal learning.

As our thoughts change toward spiritual transformation, we begin to treat everyone and every situation we come in contact with in a new way. New thinking brings new awareness and ultimately new results. Without judgment, we move away from those who do not wish to live toward spiritual growth but we realize that this is their path. We approach others with openness and nonjudgment because we begin to understand that they are not yet ready to make the transition. Ultimately, we see that some people are at one end of the continuum of *Homo nuovo* where the world is only material and perceived through the five senses. At the other end are those who are completely transformed into Spiritual Beings, but most will be somewhere in the middle. Most people will have a flicker of awareness at some point in their lives that life on this planet is more than mere survival and material gain. When this happens for each individual is unknown and it appears that it cannot be forced. Some have to experience crisis after crisis and much suffering before the mind will open to a new way of being. For others it may happen in an instant; one comment from a stranger, one glance from a home-less person, one word, and the realization is made that humans are in this experience for a higher purpose.

As we change and progress, one of the great challenges is to be mindful and respectful of the journey of others. As we begin to be filled with great love and a joy that we have not had before, others may not yet be ready for this experience. It is again with our awareness that we recognize the unique paths of others. Though we may share what we know with them from our own perspective, this may or may not be the switch that turns on the transformation. Some need to hear and see the characteristics of *Homo nuovo* in hundreds of others before they begin to understand that there is an-other way of being. The entire force of creation is helping each and every one of us to transform and when we are ready, and when all conditions are right for us, a small ray of light will begin to illuminate our minds.

CHAPTER 17

SPIRITUAL STRIDES

———

To Michael W., Geraldine O.-W., Travis M., Ken L.,
and all those who brought this book to life.

ONCE THE LIGHT of change has entered into the mind, the transformational process has begun. A Spiritual Being is in the making and if we choose to participate with it rather than push against it, it will quicken. We choose to transform at all levels of our being, as best we can, without exclusion. We also begin to see, know, and feel a different world than the one we have always perceived with our five senses alone. We see the world within the world, and begin participating with it in an entirely new way.

The transformation to a Spiritual Being becomes a way of life in every moment. Life is our practice. We cannot ignore or dismiss any instance and we know that everything matters — every little thing. With this knowledge, we bring our awareness to what shows up in our lives as best we can. Our practice does not exist solely in a church, synagogue, or temple. It does not exist only at meditation or with our family and friends or the people we love and respect. It exists with every stranger we meet on a busy street. It exists with health challenges, poverty, pain, and suffering. We are on our transformational path when we choose to live differently in our minds, journey inward to our emotions, and begin to change physically.

Connecting with like-minded people, those who are also choosing to spiritually transform, can be very helpful to us. We will know whom to connect with by their words and actions. If they are choosing actions that uplift others and themselves by not complaining, acting negatively, gossiping, or being deceitful then we can see they too are in the process of transforming. We also know by how we feel when we spend time in the company of others. If they transgress in any way but try to right the behavior and break their own deleterious patterns, then they are on the path. If we are drained, tired, or agitated in the company of certain people, then this is not in our best interest for very long. We learn what we need to learn and, hopefully, move along to better feeling circumstances. We will then feel happier, more joyful, and become immersed in love for having spent time with people who uplift us and help us to transform.

It is also very common that people in our lives will come and go as we change. As we move away from gossiping ourselves, those who still need to gossip will not want to be with us. As we stop judging and look inward, those who are similar will want to be in our presence. We no longer need to keep relationships for life but, rather, we cultivate them for our mutual learning and growth. We also let others go when they no longer need to be with us. There is an understanding that each person will get what they need from the other for their transformational progress, and for whatever time frame that may be. It could be a lifetime, a few moments, or anything in between.

Just as we choose people with awareness, we also choose places with our spiritual transformation in mind. We may find that attending church, temple, synagogue, or meditation circles uplifts us and moves us closer to the heart. In certain environments, we are moved to that feeling which animates us with a positive sense of being alive. Some places may feel warm and inviting, giving us that sense of being cared for. Other environments will feel cold and will drain us of our energy. These environments are pulling at the five senses in a negative way and should be avoided as much as possible. Again, we know by how we feel which environments are moving us in a positive direction. By going inward to our body, mind, and emotions, we are able to judge what is uplifting us and what is not. An environment that repeatedly brings on a headache is giving us the signal that this is not in our best interest at the physical level. Environments that cause anxiety or a feeling as though a blanket of darkness has come over us are nudging us at the emotional level, warning us that this is an unwanted place. Similarly, places that cause frantic thinking or disruption of thinking are signaling a place that is not healthy for the mind. By living in awareness, we come to discern what is in our best transformative interest.

With expanded awareness, the focus during transformation moves away from the self as an individual to one of feeling connected to all things, all of life, and all of creation. We no longer begin seeking things that are for our benefit only. We slowly move toward a greater awareness of how all things are connected. When we purchase a new piece of furniture, whether it is a bamboo stool or a leather chair, we can see, know, and feel all the people that are connected to that chair. When we eat a meal we have a deep connection to everyone who contributed to that meal, from the plants, animals, and farmers, to those who prepared each dish, and everyone in between.

As we transform at each level of being, we begin to surrender to the great force of life. The force that is life itself; it gives breath to a newborn baby, allows birds to fly, and fish to swim. It is the very thing that animates all things in the universe. We come to trust that this force of life is who we really are and we can let ourselves release into it.

We trust life and the process of transformation even more over time as we look inward as much as possible. We look at our thoughts that arise without letting them spin out of control. We look at our emotional landscape without attaching to any of its currents.

We look at our body and what it needs to become a clear filter for the process of change. Eventually we come to see that all of these act as a symphony, working together, to create something greater in us at the spiritual level. This is the level where we are able to become more than all of those things together. It is also the level of our being that allows us to create senses beyond what the five senses can do alone. As Spiritual Beings in human form, we become more complicated and, at the same time, begin to experience life in a more complex way than we have ever done before.

Becoming Spiritual Beings also allows us to increase our capacity for joy. This profound human emotion is allowed to resonate more fully as we provide a clear body, mind, and emotional system for it to flow through. Joy becomes the mainstay of the Spiritual Being. Life continues to occur and situations continue to arise, but the Spiritual Being sees, knows, and feels all things in a different way. Relationships stabilize and we understand why physical health is as it is. Financial situations shift and attachment to material things is modified. All of life's challenges are welcomed as transformative potential. With openness to new experiences and a new way of being human come great joy and a deep, profound love that we could not know until we had transformed.

Spiritual Beings come to experience love with every cell of their bodies and beyond. This love is not one rooted in romantic notions created in stories of make-believe but, rather, is a strong, pulsating wave with immense force. We come to know this love past our human mind and emotions into a deeper space of immense capacity. This is the force that creates life and worlds. It is the force that holds planets and galaxies together. It is the very stuff of which we are made and we come to know it in our transformed state. It is through this knowing that our lives become greater than what they could be as five-sensory humans alone.

Our new lives suddenly become orchestrated by synchronicity and come in tune with the dreaming mind. Waking-day experiences and sleep time become merged as continued life experiences. People, places, and things come into our lives exactly as we need or want them to be. These things occur with thought and feeling combined with intention. We come to participate with a life force that is guiding us through our everyday lives. The physical world begins to speak to us directly when we are aware enough to notice. People who can help us along our way will suddenly be put on our path. We will be directed to events that can guide us to where we need to go. The transformed human stays alert for signals from the environment, which act as signposts to the correct direction. We recognize guidance and truthful information by how it feels as it uplifts us and moves us in the right direction. At the same time, dreams and nighttime imagery begin to provide guidance and to speak directly to the dreamer of waking-day events. Help and assistance comes for every life problem and situation in a transformative way.

In unison with all the information that comes, we begin to communicate with the force that is guiding our lives. We communicate in a way that feels right for each and every one of us. There is no obligation, no words that must be repeated but, rather, we choose the form of communication that resonates for us. This can be in the form of prayer, music, walking in nature, or writing. Communication comes in as many forms as there are people. Some may feel the deep connection in formal religious rituals; others will feel it while gardening. As we transform and cooperate with our own transformation at each level of being, we begin to find our spiritual balance. The practice, in its multitude of forms, begins to take shape with no rules or laws of what needs to be done. What is done comes from a pull toward wanting to participate in one's own transforming life, from within.

Perhaps most importantly, the Spiritual Being lives each moment knowing that there is life after this physical life. There is also the sense that the end of life in this form is the beginning of life in the next form. We do not simply disappear after death but move to life as pure consciousness beyond or within this physical world. We know it and live our lives with this knowing. Everyday life then takes on a new meaning. What we do in each and every moment is carving and creating the being that will move to the next form of existence. How we treat others, the attitude we have about our work, the way we treat children, the life we live in our minds and emotions; all of this we take forward into the next phase of life. When we know this we become cognizant of what we do in every moment, as best we can. We do this because we have the desire to become better forms of life here and beyond. We know we are creating ourselves with the choices we make and we do this with awareness and a deep sense of love.

As we continue to change and practice we also become aware that we will continue to change when it is time. Part of the transformational process is to know that this is never-ending so we become flexible in our practice. In order to keep moving forward we may change our practice as we need to. As our conscious awareness expands, we can accept more information and new practices that are compatible with our level of learning. Since we are forever expanding, we are never at the destination as the journey of spiritual transformation continues forever.

Spiritual Beings expand at every level and with every fiber of their being; a personal and private path of transformation is created. We never ask, cajole, or push others in joining us since this is our path as we see it. People may begin to observe that we live life differently and become curious as to how this is so. They may see we are less apt to anger in the workplace. They may notice that we are particularly close to our children at all stages of their development. They may also begin to feel peaceful and fulfilled for having shared time with us and begin to wonder why this is so. Upon inquiry, this may be the time to share what we know and how we have evolved into Spiritual Beings.

By sharing our stories with others they can begin to see that a new way of life is possible. They may also begin to see parts of their own lives reflected back to them in some way. A woman may share that she began caring for her physical body and developing a ritual of prayer. The result was her inner life changing and synchronicity beginning to occur for her. She can share with others how events occurred at exactly the right moment in time that changed her entire life. A man may begin his practice with yoga and then find himself having precognitive dreams. He shares that his dream life began giving him direction about his work so he could help others with their professional and private lives. Though each individual will have a spiritual path in their own way, there will also be similarities and parallel paths with others. Sharing experiences will validate our path but also help us develop a community for transformative involvement.

As we progress along the path of *Homo nuovo* or the Spiritual Being, we develop a strong sense of identity that is based on something that unites us with all other people. We become aware of a connection between our own life force and that of all living things. We eventually see ourselves extended into everything else with our thoughts, feelings, and behaviors throughout the universe, via the domino effect. We are able to be unique individuals with our own spiritual identity and, at the same time, feel completely connected to all of creation.

As we transform with each and every step in our practice, we begin to live with little or no suffering. Though life continues to happen, we choose thoughts, feelings, and behaviors that do not create pain. We keep our focus on our inner journey, which takes us to a place of living life with deep joy and love. Eventually more and more time is spent this way so no matter what is happening in the physical world, an intense love for all that is happening is felt. There is an acceptance that these things are what they are: expressions of creation.

Another marker for the Spiritual Being is the immense thankfulness for life and all it brings. This felt sense comes from deep within and literally emanates from every cell. The profound sense of gratefulness comes when the body begins to change in response to spiritual transformation. This extends to the mind when we are able to make it peaceful from our practice. Again, deep in our emotional lives, we become able to settle the tidal waves of rampant emotion and the appreciation for this calm and joyful state resonates throughout. As we see the glorious symphony of events and people interacting with our own five senses to create a greater way of experiencing the world, we are brought to humility and thanks in a way we have never experienced before. When we resonate with joy we have become the force of love itself, and we are deeply grateful for this new way of living because we know that a Spiritual Being has emerged.

EPILOGUE

OVER A SPAN of approximately seventeen years, I began irrevocable, life-altering changes physically, emotionally, mentally, and spiritually that I did not understand, nor could I stop. This transformation was very dramatic but more importantly, I came to learn that I was just one of many, if not millions, on the planet undergoing a similar transformation. This metamorphosis was occurring for people of all ages and cultures globally, and had been going on for millennia.

Initially, I did not know why these changes were occurring but I felt very different inside my own body in ways that I could not initially articulate. At the time, my life appeared very normal at many levels; I was a university professor, researcher, and author. I was also a mother of two boys, a wife, colleague, a daughter, a sister, and a friend. I appeared to be living a life without any extraordinary experiences or circumstances. I worked hard, spent time with people I loved, and pursued my personal hobbies and interests. Despite that, my transformation from a person who lived and perceived the world through the five senses to one who developed into a more complicated and spiritually centered being seemed destined to occur. No matter what I did, life situations were forcing me to see the world differently and to accept an entirely new way of being. Though I did not knowingly initiate the changes and even at times actively tried to stop them from occurring, they were going to occur with or without my consent.

What happened to me was a dramatic change where I began to feel other people's feelings and the intentions underlying their behavior. I would look at someone and could feel why they were saying what they were saying or doing what they were doing. I could literally reach into a person's emotional life and read what was churning inside of them. A deep and profound connection to people was developing for me in a way that I had not experienced before.

In one of my earliest revelations, I began thinking about traveling to India to share my work and to explore the country. Shortly thereafter I sat beside a man at a professional conference who happened to be the organizer for an upcoming conference in India on spirituality and psychology; after a few moments of discussion he asked if I would like to participate as a speaker in New Delhi, India. These were the early signs that something new was occurring in my life, which alerted me to pay attention. I was beginning to see, know, and feel the world around me in a different way. I could see, know, and feel important life events unraveling from a greater perspective and I was waking up to something completely new.

As time went on and I continued to pay attention, I developed an ability to "see through" people in ways that I could not always understand. This ability began to extend to people I did not know or feel connected to in any way. The information appeared rather randomly as I began seeing and feeling situations that were occurring for them in their lives such as strong emotional experiences, extramarital affairs, or even illness in the body.

In one instance, I was acquainted with a woman whom I had not met before. We were briefly introduced and I was told that she was married and had a young son; when we shook hands I felt a jolt of emotional turmoil and intense pain from inside her. At the time I could not understand what this was but over a period of a few years the feelings became clearer. There was confusion, anger, hatred, and avoidance emanating from her being whenever I was in her presence. Though she appeared on the outside to be happily married and connected to her son I came to understand the emotions as repulsion to her family and a draw toward another man. Shortly thereafter, she left her husband and son for a man whom she had been secretly involved with in a romantic way.

I also developed an interesting phenomenon related to people's health problems. I would walk into a hospital room to visit a friend and could feel the aura of death lingering over the person. If this essence came to me they would die within several days. It also happened out in public where I would see a woman in the grocery store or a man walking down the street and feel the aura of death emanating from them. This sensing of new information became so strong and so loud that I could no longer deny it. I was changing and I was seeing, knowing, and feeling the world in which I lived in a whole new way.

A significant change that also occurred was that I began having precognitive dreams. I would dream about events, in every detail, a day or two ahead of the waking-day events occurring. The dreams were short, vivid, and very clear. I would dream specific details about people, some I had not yet met. I would dream about places and events that would then occur in my waking life in the exact detail of the dream. I would also dream about other people's health issues or waking-life situations in ways that I could not possibly have known about. Eventually, my dreams were only precognitive in nature and all other forms of dreaming ceased to occur.

Another phenomenon that developed was a voice coming to me during sleep with guidance and answers to my life situations. The voice would not wake me but would give very clear direction for my waking-day life. The guidance was unmistakeable and when I followed the direction that was given, it was never wrong.

As all of this was happening I also found myself unable to tolerate certain kinds of foods, noises, and chemicals. As a result, a terrible and insidious illness developed under certain environmental conditions. I had to become completely aware of my surroundings and the people in it so I would not become overloaded with physical and extrasensory stimulation to the point of becoming ill.

As all of these changes continued, a wonderful shift simultaneously occurred where I began to feel a connection to people and to all things in the universe in a deep and profound way that I had never experienced before. Incredible feelings of joy and love were felt. These emotions emanated from within me and were not connected to any one person or thing. The intensity of joy and love increased and were not romantic or contained in any way; the connection intensified as the years passed and this great source of love kept growing inside of me. When I felt someone's pain I could also feel love for them no matter what they were doing or why they were doing it. I also came to understand that love is embedded in all things, no matter how it looks or feels to our five senses.

The newly realized changes were continual and I finally delved into trying to understand what was happening to me by reading voraciously and meeting people who could possibly offer explanations.

This brought forth people who had undergone similar changes and could see, know, and feel the same things that I was experiencing but to an even greater extent. The process of change continued to bring about great physical, mental, emotional, and spiritual transformations that enriched my life at every possible level. Life became more fulfilling and meaningful than I could have ever imagined and I learned that I was not alone.

Perhaps the most wonderful revelation is that no matter where we are in the journey to becoming a Spiritual Being, it has always just begun and there is much more to come; it is the grandest adventure of life. We are all simply on the way to becoming more than what we are while being a part of something so vast that we cannot know it fully; we can merely experience it. The time for us to experience this has come and for those of us who are transforming en masse, we can accept this transformation as the new norm. We fully accept who we are and then we live it and share it as best we can.

ABOUT THE AUTHOR

CAT ZECHNER

TERESA L. DECICCO, PHD was a university professor, researcher, and author studying Dreams and Dreaming and Psychology of the Spiritual Self when a wave of spiritual transformative experiences occurred. From then on, over a seventeen-year period, her experience with near death, clairsentience, precognitive dreaming, and other transformations led her to understand the spiritual transformation that was occurring, not only in her, but in millions of others at this time in history. Dr. DeCicco wrote *Living Beyond the Five Senses* after transformations led her to see, know, and feel existence beyond the five senses alone. This book is for seekers of the soul who do not wish to adopt religious doctrine or new age spirituality, but rather, wish to find their own personal spiritual balance.

Dr. DeCicco welcomes comments, sharing of personal experiences, and questions about becoming a Spiritual Being at tdecicco1@rogers.com. Information and updates on talks and seminars can be found at www.teresadecicco.org, on Facebook, LinkedIn, and her blog: www.livingbeyondthefivesenses.com.

When she is not traveling, she lives in Canada, spending time between the provinces of Ontario and Quebec with her husband, where she skis, hikes, cycles, cooks, gardens, and enjoys the company of her two grown boys.

HERE ARE OTHER **DIVINE ARTS** BOOKS YOU MAY ENJOY

DIVINE
ARTS

THE SACRED SITES OF THE DALAI LAMAS
Glenn H. Mullin   2013 Nautilus Silver Medalist

"As this most beautiful book reveals, the Dalai Lamas continue to teach us that there are, indeed, other ways of thinking, other ways of being, other ways of orienting ourselves in social, spiritual, and ecological space."
— Wade Davis, Explorer-in-Residence, National Geographic Society

THE SHAMAN & AYAHUASCA: *Journeys to Sacred Realms*
Don José Campos   2013 Nautilus Silver Medalist

"This remarkable and beautiful book suggests a path back to under-standing the profound healing and spiritual powers that are here for us in the plant world. This extraordinary book shows a way toward reawakening our respect for the natural world, and thus for ourselves."
— John Robbins, author, *The Food Revolution* and *Diet for a New America*

A HEART BLOWN OPEN: *The Life & Practice of Zen Master Jun Po Denis Kelly Roshi*
Keith Martin-Smith   2013 Nautilus Silver Medalist

"This is the story of our time... an absolute must-read for anyone with even a passing interest in human evolution..."
— Ken Wilber, author, *Integral Spirituality*

"This is the legendary story of an inspiring teacher that mirrors the journey of many contemporary Western seekers."
— Alex Grey, artist and author of *Transfigurations*

SOPHIA—THE FEMININE FACE OF GOD: *Nine Heart Paths to Healing and Abundance*
Karen Speerstra   2013 Nautilus Gold Medalist

"Karen Speerstra shows us most compellingly that when we open our hearts, we discover the wisdom of the Feminine all around us. A totally refreshing exploration, and beautifully researched read."
— Michael Cecil, author, *Living at the Heart of Creation*

NEW BELIEFS NEW BRAIN: *Free Yourself from Stress and Fear*
Lisa Wimberger

"Lisa Wimberger has earned the right, through trial by fire, to be regarded as a rising star among meditation teachers. No matter where you are in your journey, New Beliefs, New Brain will shine a light on your path."
— Marianne Williamson, author, *A Return to Love* and *Everyday Grace*

ONWARD & UPWARD: *Reflections of a Joyful Life*
Michael Wiese

"Onward & Upward is the memoir of a rare and wonderful man, who has lived a truly extraordinary life. It's filled with Michael Wiese's adventures, his incredible journeys, and his interactions with amazing people."
— John Robbins, author, *Diet for a New America*, co-founder: Food Revolution Network

A FULLER VIEW: *Buckminster Fuller's Vision of Hope and Abundance for All*
L. Steven Sieden

"This book elucidates Buckminster Fuller's thinking, honors his spirit, and creates an enthusiasm for continuing his work."
— Marianne Williamson, author, *Return To Love* and *Healing the Soul of America*

A SHAMAN'S TALE: *Path to Spirit Consciousness*
Richard L. Alaniz

"Inspiring and life-changing wisdom, A Shaman's Tale provides the reader with a unique perspective in fulfilling their spiritual consciousness."
— Al Diaz, author, *The Titus Concept: Money For My Best and Highest Good*, *Being The Titus Concept*, and *Confirmations*

HEAL YOUR SELF WITH WRITING
Catherine Ann Jones

"This is so much more than a book on writing. It is a guide to the soul's journey, with Catherine Ann Jones as a compassionate teacher and wise companion along the way."
— Dr. Betty Sue Flowers, Series Consultant/Editor, *Joseph Campbell and the Power of Myth*

RECIPES FOR A SACRED LIFE: *True Stories and a Few Miracles*
Rivvy Neshama

"Neshama's stories are uplifting, witty, and wise: one can't go wrong with a recipe like that. The timeless wisdom she serves up is food for the soul."
— *Publisher's Weekly*

GARDENS OF THE SOUL: *Making Sacred and Shamanic Art*
Faith Nolton

"Faith Nolton's book is wonderful and beautiful, with paintings and text that only come from a deep understanding of shamanic experience."
— Michael Harner, author, *The Way of the Shaman* and *Cave and Cosmos*

Divine Arts sprang to life fully formed
as an intention to bring spiritual practice
into daily life.

*Human beings are far more than the one-dimensional creatures perceived
by most of humanity and held static in consensus reality. There is a deep
and vast body of knowledge — both ancient and emerging — that informs
and gives us the understanding, through direct experience, that we are
magnificent creatures occupying many dimensions with untold powers and
connectedness to all that is.*

*Divine Arts books and films explore these realms, powers, and teachings
through inspiring, informative, and empowering works by pioneers,
artists, and great teachers from all the wisdom traditions. We invite your
participation and look forward to learning how we may serve you.*

Onward and upward,
Michael Wiese, Publisher